MW01254122

Register for our web site www.cocktailcool.com and join the growing interactive community of professionals there as we share knowledge, training techniques and most valuable of all, our experiences behind the bar.

THE COCKTAIL COOL BAR
A TEXTBOOK FOR BARTENDERS
1st EDITION

by Michael Armstrong & Ryan McClure

Cheers!

1st Edition

Published by Cocktail Cool
An imprint of Cocktail Cool, LLC
P.O. Box 370
Hanna, WY
USA

www.cocktailcool.com

Email: cocktailcool@mac.com

DEDICATED

to Kathleen and Ronald McClure,
who taught me to be academic about all things in life.

to Michelle and Brandy Armstrong,
whose faith is a reward in itself.

English Ebook ISBN 978-0-9799994-0-6

TABLE OF CONTENTS

"Civilization begins with distillation."

- William Faulkner,
20th Century American Writer

GOALS

Motivation

Empowering bartenders to encourage customers to demand quality when ordering a cocktail in a bar, as well as providing the knowledge to discern what makes a quality mixed drink.

Relationships

Distributors, liquor companies and bartenders need to work together to promote education and this requires communication. The global spirits market is fragmented further by regional disparities in available knowledge. Communication is the bridge between borders and cultures that is necessary to carry the industry into the future and provide a level playing field for all.

Responsible Action

Served in the right environment, cocktails can provide an enjoyable atmosphere with a touch of sophistication. Taxi rides should be facilitated as a transportation alternative and the entire bar staff can be encouraged to think along these lines as an element of training that directly reduces the tragedies that can result from the misuse of alcohol.

Knowledge of Brands and Products

The food and beverage industry is as old as recorded history and as internationally diverse as the world's cultures. It's complicated - to the extent that owners, sales representatives, distributors and service personnel are always hungry for knowledge of the incredible variety available in today's marketplace.

History

Cocktail culture has enjoyed a storied legacy around the world for hundreds of years. Alcohol has impacted the history of most civilizations for thousands of years. By learning the "how" and "why" bartenders can better understand today's evolved global marketplace.

Profit Margins

Understanding the bottom line is essential for owners, sales representatives, distributors and every bartender.

Responsible Drinking

The science of alcohol's effects on the human body should be common knowledge. But if a patron has had too much to drink, there needs to be a clear protocol for bartenders.

RECIPES

Our Favorite Originals

Bartenders get asked about their favorite drink all the time. While a lot of bartenders have a signature cocktail, one they really make well or created themselves, it's not necessarily their favorite cocktail to drink.

Early on in the writing of this book, we sent a draft copy to a friend who works for one of the largest spirit companies in the world. This was his reply:

"I love the way there's no branding in the whole front bit. Gives you credibility, shows your impartiality, not selling your souls (not openly anyway!), massive endorsement to read on."

Throughout this text you'll find some unique and popular bottles on display and an original recipe for each. They're all great products but none of the companies involved paid for placement, which apparently will keep our souls intact. We just thought they were special products that deserved a mention because we were able to concoct really drinkable original cocktails with them. Some of them are available all over the world, some of them can only be found in certain regions or states. Check the back of the book for a more extensive list of world famous recipes as well as our Company Brand Index so you can look beyond the marketing and see who owns what all over the world.

Enjoy.

THE BLOODY BULL
2 oz 267 Chili Pepper Tequila
3 - 5 dashes Worcestershire Sauce
2 dashes Dry Dill or Dry Herb of your choice
6 - 7 oz V-8 Juice
Garnish with celery stick and lime wedge
A Bloody Bull has a sharper taste than a Bloody Mary and the infused chili pepper make this drink an eye opener.

CULTURE

Cocktail Culture and Bottle Culture

One can never learn enough about global cultures, but a good bartender will always make the attempt. To understand contemporary cocktail culture it helps to first consider the concept of bottle culture.

Bottle culture is simple: A bottle of spirits is purchased and the patron is served with glasses, ice decanter and a variety of mixers. They pay a small fee for the mixers and service. In Asia, if there is any leftover the bottle is tagged with the patron's name and put behind the bar until they return, but at many establishments in North America leftover spirits are not kept for next time which actually encourages patrons to finish the bottle.

This situation is great for large market players and trendy new products. From a bar owner's perspective it guarantees a minimum revenue. Service personnel, not bartenders, need less training and professional ability to tend to patrons. However, it's also very conducive to heavy drinking. A bottle just sitting in the middle of the table tends to disappear a lot faster. For instance, when it comes time to toast in China, Gambai! "Dry your glass!" is heard often and is not to be taken lightly.

Presently, this is how the majority of Chinese people drink and how most bars operate across China. This practice hurts bartending and encourages the misuse of alcohol.

China wasn't always this way. There was a very sophisticated mixed drink culture present in Shanghai and Peking during the 1920's and

1930's. Shanghai was much like New York or London today, there were bartenders that knew your name, your drink and how to make it - provided you were in the right place. Many exiled Russian royals spent their days in Shanghai and Peking hotel bars, stoically creating drinks that would carry their fame and flavor around the world.

In the Shanghai of the 1930's the most popular drink was the Shanghai Buck. It took a skilled bartender to mix the bitters, grenadine, ginger ale, lime juice and rum. In fact, since the Shanghai Buck called specifically for Bacardi Rum. Bacardi sold more product in Shanghai than in any other city in the world during this period. There aren't many Chinese bars at the moment that even know the Shanghai Buck ever existed, which is forgivable if you factor in the chaos of World War II. Just as Prohibition hurt bartending as a

profession in the United States, World War II effectively killed it in China. It is still not the same profession it is elsewhere and this is a direct result of what replaced the vibrant cocktail culture of China - bottle culture. From 1920 to 1933 alcohol was illegal in the United States, a period in time known as Prohibition. Despite being a legitimate profession prior to Prohibition, bartenders were not needed at speakeasies, establishments where people gathered to drink alcohol illegally. Because of the secretive nature of speakeasies, bottle culture prevailed, and when Prohibition ended the notion of the professional American bartender had taken a serious blow.

The term bar literally means to separate the patrons from the store of alcohol. The bartender is the dispenser of spirits, but also responsible for maintaining a civilized atmosphere. The idea of bottle culture removes this responsible barrier and the professional experience bartenders provide. It also seriously limits the selection of tastes available to patrons.

The impact of bottle culture on the profession of bartending has been detrimental in the past, although today it is being toted as a viable new business model for bars. While VIP bottle service can rake-in more revenue in certain establishments, a properly run Service Bar can provide the same revenue while maintaining the responsible environment required for the consumption of spirits and providing the full spectrum of mixed drinks that have evolved over the centuries.

From the 20s & 30s

Astor Hotel Special- Shanghai, 1926

Broken Spur- Peking, 1932

Imperial Cossack Crusta- Shanghai, 1930's

Far Eastern Gimlet- From from Hong Kong to Bombay

Tiger's Milk- Peking, 1931

Rosy Dawn Cocktail- Canton, 1930's

Russian Cocktail- Grande de Hotel of Peking, 1926

The Famous Shanghai Buck- 1930's

Check Page 63 for these classic recipes.

Check Page 63 for these classic recipes.

"**Melancholy, indeed, should be diverted by every means but drinking.**"

- Samual Johnson,
18th Century English Essayist / Moralist

HISTORY

The Cocktail

Most mixed drinks are referred to as cocktails. However, this grouping is relatively new. Before the 1950's, mixed drinks were divided into groups by their ingredients or serving requirements. For example, Flips always have an egg as an ingredient and this sets them apart. Juleps, Fizzes, Slings, Crustas, Cocktails, Daisies, Bucks, Rickeys and Fixes are all different categories of mixed drinks that go back hundreds of years. They have only recently been rolled into the one word - cocktail.

So where did the term cocktail come from? No one knows for sure, but there are some lively stories worth noting.

One story is that Betsy Flanagan coined the phrase. An American patriot who owned a bar next door to a chicken farm in Yorktown, New York. In 1779, Betsy's Tavern was a meeting place for American and French officers in George Washington's army. The popular drink of the day was a blend of rums, fruit brandies and whatever mixer was available. The drink was called a Bracer.

The officers would make fun of Betsy's neighbor and all of his excellent chickens because he was a British Loyalist. She threatened they would eat their words one day. Although no true American patriot would buy from a British Loyalist, she had a chicken feast for the American and French officers and then had them retire to the bar where they could drink their Bracers.

Betsy had decorated each glass with a cock's tail from the offending neighbor's birds. A toast was given to the "cocktail" in amusement and the name stuck.

A slightly less specific tale is that in the Southern United States, in the early 1800's, people would start drinking as they started their day. Thus, all drinks imbibed in the morning were given the name cocktail in honor of the cock's morning announcement.

There are so many creation myths that identifiying the lineage of the word is conjeceture at best, the point is, at one time cocktail referred to a specific category of mixed drink - not all mixed drinks.

Spirits Throughout History

Whether for medicinal, ceremonial or just to be social, humans and alcohol have been intimately involved since the beginning of recorded history. Here are just a few interesting facts to bring up at your next cocktail party regarding spirits throughout more recent human history.

Christopher Columbus took sugarcane to the New World in 1493 on his second voyage. His trial plantings were made on the Caribbean island of Santo Domingo, modern day Dominican Republic/Haiti. He quickly reported to Queen Isabella of Spain that it grew better here than anywhere in Europe and thus began sugarcane's long and storied history in the Caribbean. Rum was soon to follow. Sadly, rum trading served to perpetuate the slave trade in this area as rum made from refined sugarcane was used to pay for the slaves who were forced to work the sugarcane plantations.

The Proof is in the Gunpowder: Before making distilled spirits became a science, the old fashioned method to measure strength was to take equal parts of spirit and gunpowder and apply a flame. If the gunpowder failed to burn, the spirit was too weak. If it burned too brightly, it was too strong. If it burned evenly, with a blue flame, it was said to be "proved".

Gin Lore
In 1650, Dr. Sylvius, a professor at the University of Lieden, Netherlands, sought a cure for the tropical diseases affecting sailors on their trips for the Dutch East India Company. Dr. Sylvius' aqua vitae came from the juniper berry and it was called jenever by his countrymen. The British discovered the spirit during the 30 Years War. They called it Dutch Courage because soldiers seemed more eager to go into battle after drinking it. Taking it back to England, they shortened the name to jen which became gin . By the turn of the eighteenth century there were over 7,000 gin shops in London.

Gin was mixed with Angostura Bitters to help relieve the symptoms of tropical diseases in India. Gin didn't work as a cure, but mixed with tonic water it was a great way to take your daily dose of Quinine, which was effective against malaria. Dr. James Lind discovered that limes prevented scurvy. English gin was later known as London Dry Gin. Holland Gin has a different, thicker taste than London Dry Gin and it has a stronger essence of juniper berry.

A Little More Refined
In the 1860's, Louis Pasteur defined fermentation as anaerobic life – life without air. In 1897, Edward Buchner reported that yeasts could be scientifically categorized and their effects on sugars could be isolated. Since then, chemistry has identified many different yeasts and documented their effects on different sugars. This is the main reason there are so many different types of spirits in the world today.

BLACK FOREST SHOT
1/2 to 1 oz of Monin Cherry Syrup
1 1/2 to 2 oz of favorite Mozart Chocolate (Black, Gold, White)
Monin Syrups are key to great tasting shots. They don't contain any alcohol, just a healthy blast of flavour.

BAR ERAS

The Gothic Era of Bartending

The era of drink from 1775 to 1865 was a time when the spirit's strength was the gage of quality. Stomachs must have been quite strong. The term comes from H.L. Mencken in his book *The American Language*,

"In the Gothic age of American Drinking and word making, between the American Revolution and the Civil War, many fantastic drinks were invented, and given equally fantastic names; stone fence, blue blazer, and stinkibus…. The touring Englishmen of those days always spread news of such grotesque drink names, some of these Columbuses embellished the list with outlandish invention of their own…"

Industrial technology was having a precipitating effect on production processes as traditional methods tried to keep up. In the 1820's Scottish whiskey was stored in barrels for the first time and the invention of the very efficient Coffey Still in 1830 allowed large-scale industrial distillation. Many communal drinks were popular and the punch bowl flowed.

Black Velvet- 4 oz of champagne or sparkling wine, 1 oz Guinness Stout Beer or a similar dark beer.

Fish House Punch- 36 oz of dark rum, 24 oz of lemon juice, 25 oz of brandy, 4 oz of peach brandy, 60 oz of sugar water - makes 30 servings.

Tom and Jerry- 1 1/2 oz of bourbon, rye or brandy, 3/4 oz rum, 1 teaspoon superfine sugar, 1 dash allspice, 1 egg, hot milk, - this is a technical drink that requires the egg yolk to be separated from the whites. Mix all the ingredients, including the egg yolk but not the egg white, and milk. Whip egg white until it stiffens, combine, then add hot milk to taste.

The Golden Age of American Bartending

The era of drink from 1865 to 1900 was a time just as good as it sounds. This term comes from *The American Language*,

"-the new drinks of the 1865-1900 era, were largely eponymous and hence relatively decorous, e.g., Rickeys and Tom Collins."

It is a commonly held belief that the Manhattan was created for American socialite Jennie Jerome, at a Manhattan party in 1874. Although, history does record her at home November 30 of this year, in Blenheim Castle, England, where she was giving birth to the future Sir Winston Churchill.

Manhattan- 1 1/2 oz of whiskey, 3/4 oz sweet vermouth, 2 dashes bitters. Shake and strain into a chilled Cocktail glass, add cherry. To make it dry use dry vermouth and garnish with a lemon twist or olive.

Astoria- 1/3 oz gin, 2/3 oz sweet vermouth, 2 dashes orange bitters. Stir with cracked ice and serve immediately.

Gimlet- 1 1/2 oz of gin, 1/2 oz Rose's Lime Juice. Garnish with a lime wedge.

The Old School Era of Bartending

The era from 1900 to 1919 ushered-in such classic drinks as the Aviation and the Mojito. Grand hotels around the world like the Waldorf Astoria in New York and the Savoy in London were home to professional bartenders, their creative talents were fostered and their inventions compared to sophisticated works of art.

Mojito- 2 to 3 oz of light rum, 1 oz fresh lime juice, 1/2 oz simple syrup, 6-8 sprigs of mint, soda - a technical drink that requires the mint to be muddled. Add the sugar, then rum, crushed ice, lime juice and fill with soda.

Side Car- 1 1/2 oz of cognac, 3/4 oz Cointreau, 1/4 oz lemon juice. Put in shaker with ice, stir, strain.

Rose- 2 oz gin, 3/4 oz Grand Marnier, put in shaker with ice, stir, strain.

> **"What's the use of winning the Nobel Prize if doesn't even get you into speakeasies?"**
>
> *- Sinclair Lewis, 20th Century American Novelist winner of the Nobel Prize for Literature*

Prohibition

In the United States from 1920 to 1933 Federal law prohibited the manufacture, transportation or sale of spirits. Herbert Hoover, the President at the time, called it the Noble Experiment. Most agree it did little to hamper spirit consumption and instead created a brand new criminal element to society. Bootlegging (the illegal sale of spirits) became big business. Law enforcement agencies were frustrated by moonshiners (illegal producers), rum-runners (spirit smugglers from the sea) and speakeasies (places where patrons drank illegally). Many spirit drinkers switched to bathtub gin (dangerous homemade gin) and mixed it with anything that would take the strong taste away. Speakeasies often had legitimate business facades like barbershops and ice cream parlors and catered to men and women but there is a notion that the speakeasy hurt the profession of bartending. The crowd that came to these places brought their own bootleg liquor hidden on their bodies, while barbacks distributed "setups" of glasses, ice and soda. There was little demand for professional bartenders.

During Prohibition there were 300,000 people convicted of breaking alcohol related laws. The federal prison population increased six-fold and $40 billion was spent on bootlegged spirits. 50,000 people were killed, blinded, or paralyzed from bad liquor. However, during all of this there were some classic cocktails born. On December 5, 1933 the United States ended Prohibition.

Floridita- 1 1/2 oz of light rum, 1/2 oz lime juice, 1/2 oz sweet vermouth, dash white crème de cacao, dash grenadine. Put in shaker with ice, stir, strain.

Leap Year- 2 oz of gin, 1/2 oz sweet vermouth, 1/2 oz Grand Marnier, 1/4 oz lemon juice. Put in shaker with ice, stir, strain.

Monkey Gland- 1 1/2 oz of gin, 1 1/2 oz of orange juice, dash anisette, 1/4 oz grenadine. Put in shaker with ice, stir, strain.

The Years of Reform

The era from 1934 to 1949. Fallout from the Prohibition era manifested itself during this period of scarce professional bartenders: not many new drinks. According to *The Old Waldorf-Astoria Bar Book*,

"the art of mixing cocktails as known and practiced up to 1919 lapsed into a sort of desuetude, even if that could not be described as 'innocuous' or even innoxious."

That might be a little harsh, especially considering these popular classics came from this period.

Diablo- 1 1/2 oz of tequila, 3/4 oz crème de casis,
1/2 oz lime juice, ginger ale. Put in shaker with ice, stir, strain into Collins glass with ice.

Mai Tai- 1 oz light rum, 3/4 ounce lime juice,
1/2 oz orange curacao, splash orgeat syrup,
4 oz of pineapple juice. Put in shaker with ice, stir, strain into Tropical glass with ice and float 3/4 oz dark rum on top.

Moscow Mule- Build in a Collins glass with ice.
1 1/2 oz of vodka, dash bitters, 1 oz lime juice,
4-6 oz of ginger ale with lime wedge.

**Don't drink to get drunk.
Drink to enjoy life.**

- Jack Kerouac, 20th Century American Writer

The Rat Pack Era

From 1955 to 1968 there was a step-back to the classics. There were not many new cocktails created and the few new drinks, like the Vesper Martini for instance, were a product of on-screen popular culture. Hollywood star swingers drank cocktails. Legend has it, Humphrey Bogart's wife, Lauren Bacall came up with the phrase "rat pack" to describe the regular guests at their late-night Holmby Hills parties: Frank Sinatra, Judy Garland, Spencer Tracy and more were regular guests. Frank Sintra later created his own, more famous Rat Pack with Dean Martin and Sammy Davis Jr.

Vesper Martini- 2 oz Gin, 1 oz vodka, 1/2 oz Lillet. Put in shaker with ice. Chill and strain into a Martini glass. Serve with an orange twist.

Harvey Wallbanger- 1 3/4 oz vodka, 2/3 oz Galliano, 5-6 oz orange juice. Serve in a Collins glass and garnish with an orange wheel.

Blue Lagoon- 1 oz vodka, 1 oz blue curacao, 5-6 oz lemonade. Serve in a Tropical glass and garnish with a lime.

I can't help myself. I'm for anything that gets you through the night, be it prayer, tranquilizers or a bottle of Jack Daniel's.

- Frank Sinatra, 20th Century Actor, Singer

The Dark Age of Bartending

1969 to 1989 is a time many pure bartenders would like to forget. Good cocktails did come out of this era, the Cosmopolitan, Caeser and Lemon Drop to name a few. However, this was the time of disco and fern bars, where the popular cocktails were sweet drinks that hid the essence of the spirit's taste. The classics were almost forgotten by the young generation that was looking to break away from the establishment.

Caesar- Build in a Tumbler glass. 1 1/2 oz of Vodka, 4 oz of Clamatto juice, dash of Worcestershire, 2 dashes Tobasco, dash celery salt, dash pepper, add diced cucumber. Celery salt the rim and garnish with a celery stick.

Cosmopolitan- 1 1/2 oz of Vodka, 3/4 oz Cointreau, 1/2 oz lime juice, splash of Ocean Spray Cranberry Juice. Put in shaker with ice, stir, strain into a Martini glass.

Fuzzy Navel- Build in a Collins glass. 1 1/2 oz Peach Schnapps, 4-6 oz of orange juice. Stir.

Lemon Drop- 1 1/2 oz of Citrus Vodka, 3/4 oz lemon juice, 1 teaspoon of simple sugar. Rim the Martini glass with sugar. Put in shaker with ice, stir, strain into Martini glass.

Sex on the Beach- Build in a Collins glass. 1 oz Midori, 1 oz Chambord, 4-6 oz of pineapple juice. Stir.

Imagination & Product Knowledge are the keys to creating new drinks

The Neo Cocktail Era

In the last two decades people all over the world have rediscovered the classics and revived the cocktail party. In addition, luxury brands have started to take-hold in bars and the retail marketplace as health-conscious consumers gravitate towards quality over quantity. Bartenders trade new recipes and techniques over the Internet and the use of fresh fruit and quality drink mixers is widespread in the better establishments around the world. The art of the cocktail has come back.

TROPICAL ORCHID
1 oz Orchid Mango Liqueur
1 oz Orchid Passion Fruit
6 oz Ocean Spray Cranberry
Splash Soda
The spirits from Orchid are made from fresh fruit and it shows in the taste of these products.

SCIENCE

Science Keywords

Some basic vocabulary used around the laboratory.

1.1
Neutral Spirits – Distilled alcohol

1.2
Potable Spirits – Drinkable spirits

1.3
Proof – A traditional measure of alcohol content two times the percentage of alcohol

2.1
Hangover – Discomfort brought on by alcohol not burned as energy by the body

Lactic Acid – A by-product of normal energy production in the body

3.1
Fermentation – Chemical change that produces alcohol from sugar

3.2
Yeast – A living plant organism that changes sugar into alcohol and carbon dioxide

Anaerobic Life – Life without air

3.3
Starch – A complex carbohydrate which is insoluble in water

Germination – The first stage in the development of a plant from a seed

Malt – Starch that has been converted into sugar.

1.1 Neutral Spirits
Neutral spirits are colorless and have no taste or smell. Alcohol distilled from grain at high temperatures creates a raw product that is 95% alcohol. Neutral spirits are used for blending and must be diluted before drinking.

1.2 Potable Spirits

Potable means drinkable. Potable spirits take on the original flavor of the solids used in distillation such as malt or fruit. Potable spirits are distilled at a lower temperature than neutral spirits. The lower the distillation temperature, the more flavor retained in the distilled spirit. As a rule of thumb, as the distillation temperature increases, so does the alcohol content, while the amount of flavoring agents decrease.

1.3 The Proof

Proof is the traditional measure for the strength of the alcohol in a distilled spirit. Proof is determined by doubling the percentage of alcohol by volume. Each degree of proof is equal to .5% alcohol. A spirit of 90 proof contains 45% alcohol. A spirit of 150 proof contains 75% alcohol. A spirit of more than 100 proof is known as an overproof spirit.

When mixing a drink it is important to note the amount of alcohol present. An overproof alcohol can be disguised by a mixer, causing the consumer to believe the drink isn't very strong when it might contain the same amount of alcohol as three or more regular cocktails. Understanding proof and percentage of alcohol is just as important as understanding taste.

> **"Claret is the liquor for boys, port for men; but he who aspires to be a hero, must drink brandy."**
>
> *- Samuel Johnson, 18th Century English Writer*

HOT ROYAL ORANGE
2 ounces of Grand Marnier
6 - 7 ounces of heated Orange Juice
A popular alternative to coffee or tea based cocktails.

2.0 Effects on the Body

Alcohol produces energy without taxing the body because it is taken into the bloodstream in its original state. The part of the body most quickly and directly affected by alcohol is the brain. Again, understanding the proof of the drink can make a big difference in how much and how fast spirits are intended to be consumed.

The best protection against the effects of drinking too much is food to line the stomach walls. The most effective foods contain butter, meat fats or olive oil.

2.1 Hangover

A hangover is the accumulation of residual lactic acid in the muscles. Lactic acid normally occurs in the body as a waste product of energy production. Any alcohol not burned-off as energy produces excess lactic acid that can only be removed via the kidneys. This process cannot be expedited and the only cure is rest and time.

Moderate consumption for relaxation or at social events can contribute to the enjoyment of the good life. Like other forms of sophisticated recreation, a proper understanding of the basics goes a long way to being responsible.

3.0 Fermentation and Distillation

The active ingredient in any type of spirit is alcohol. Alcohol is produced from sugar or from a product that can first be made into sugar. Once there is sugar, it can be transformed into alcohol by the natural process of fermentation.

**"Let us have wine and women, mirth and laughter,
Sermons and soda water, the day after."**

- George Gordon, Lord Byron, 18th Century English Poet

Ethanol

Dextrin

Maltose

3.1 Fermentation

Fermentation is a chemical change. A single molecule of sugar is split into two molecules of ethyl alcohol and two molecules of carbon dioxide gas. The gas escapes into the air and the alcohol remains. The agent of fermentation is yeast. Ethyl alcohol is also known as ethanol.

3.2 Yeast

Yeast is a living plant organism capable of self-reproduction. It has many individual strains, and a different scientific name for each. Alcoholic fermentation only occurs naturally in the presence of small living yeasts.

3.3 Malt

Starch can be converted into sugar using malt. Commercial spirits are usually produced from grain products like corn, wheat or potatoes because malt can turn their inexpensive starch into valuable sugar. Grain is submerged in water to begin germination. It is then dried in a kiln. The result is called malt, and the principle enzyme in malt is called amylase. Amylase converts starch into the sugars dextrin and maltose. After this process is complete, yeasts can convert these sugars into alcohol.

DISTILLATION

Distillation

The principle behind distillation is that alcohol vaporizes and becomes a gas at a lower temperature than water. The boiling point of water is 100 C after which it becomes steam. The boiling point of ethyl alcohol is 78.333 C. So if a liquid that contains alcohol is heated and the temperature is kept under 100 C, the alcohol will separate from the original liquid into vapor. If contained in an apparatus that allows no vapor to escape, it can be recondensed into a liquid form. The result is a higher purity alcohol. To make this product drinkable takes a master distiller or a recipe that has been honed over time.

The very first rising vapors and the last condensing droplets of alcohol are called feintes or heads and tails. The feintes are considered less pure and are thrown away.

Commercial distillation results in a mixture that never goes above 192 proof or 96% alcohol. 200 proof can only be made under laboratory conditions. Because of its high purity, no matter what the source, sugarcane, grape or grain; at this point it all tastes the same. Neutral spirits seldom go above 190 proof and are used mostly for blending. Blending is the marrying of two or more similar products to obtain a spirit of a more uniform quality.

Now I, friend, drink to you, friend,
As my friend drank to me,
And I, friend, charge you, friend,
As my friend charged me,
That you, friend, drink to your friend,
As my friend drank to me;
And the more we drink together, friend,
The merrier we'll be.

- Toast - Anonymous

CATDADDY ON THE ROCKS
Spicy, just slightly sweet
put it on the rocks - it is made for sipping.

MATURATION

Aging

Drinkable spirits have different product names. More than the product names, the characteristics that make them different from one another are the flavoring elements, how they are stored and for how long.

In the process known as aging, the spirit matures in a wooden vessel undergoing changes in its composition that develop its flavor. As long as the alcohol is in wood, there is constant chemical change because of oxidation from the air in the barrel and the interaction with the wood. The length of time spent in this oxidation reaction results in different congener levels. Congeners in spirits consist of:

Acids found in spirits vary, but include prop ionic, butyric, tartaric, lactic, succinic and others.

Fusel Oils are a complex mixture of higher alcohols, mainly propyl, butyl, amyl, hexyl, heptyl and the dialcohols, trialcohols and their reactive products.

Esters are produced by the chemical combination of the acids and the alcohols. They are the substances that give aroma to a spirit.

Aldehydes are produced by the combination of the alcohols and air. They contribute the most to a spirit's character and taste.

In the wooden vessel the spirit also absorbs **tannin** and other coloring compounds from the wood. It becomes less harsh and markedly sweeter. There is a certain loss of alcohol in the barrel due to evaporation. This lost product is known as the Angel's Share.

Master Distillers must be able to consistently measure the spirit at all times to ensure that the product going into the glass vessel is perfect, as once the oxidation reaction is stopped *the taste will not change.*

THE BAR

The Front Bar and the Service Bar

There are two basic types of bars, the Front bar where the drinks are made in-front of the customer and the Service bar designed strictly for wait staff. Sometimes a Service bar is called the Back bar because it's out-of-sight. The lay-out of either bar is important to the speed and efficiency of operations.

The Front Bar

A Front bar is all about sales. The key to a successful Front bar is how well the bottles are displayed. This is an opportunity to show your wares and display area amounts to prime-real estate for brands and bottles. A bar that neglects the presentation of brands is damaging sales.

Ideally, staff should be graduates of a quantifiable training program. A Front bar usually has different working stations for bar personnel. Bar staff may have apprenticed under a talented bartender or studied the art of making cocktails in school. Either way, they should be well versed on the products and services they provide and be good with customers. People skills are just as important as mixing skills at a Front bar. A good understanding of crowd dynamics is crucial to Front bar layout. Front bars are where sales can jump if the right staff and supplies are on-hand.

In many cases, new establishments forget to take into consideration the long hours a bartender puts in behind a Front bar. Wooden racks on the floor or cushioned rubber mats make a huge difference to bartender ergonomics and a more comfortable bartender means an increase in productivity.

The working space for bartenders should be large enough for at least two people to get by comfortably. Any design layout should focus on the placement of the sink, refrigerators and access to ice. There should be counter-top space available for chopping and easy access to plumbing in case repairs need to be made.

> "The Cocktail is intended to be like unto a bugle call to meals: it must not be sweet, nor warm, nor long, nor soft, but on the contrary, in order to whet the appetite as well as stimulate conversation, it should be flavoursome, cold, spirity, and served in small glasses, one sip or two, and no more."
>
> *- Andre Simon,*
> *Early 20th Century French Wine Merchant*

The Service Bar

A Service bar can be out-of-sight, so bottle placement should focus on convenience and speed. A Service bar is used in restaurants and hotels that often host banquets and other large volume functions. A Service bar is set-up for supplying drinks quickly, not public relations. The system and the bartenders should focus on getting the drinks out fast and with consistent taste.

The Front bar and Service bar can be combined, but what the public sees is important. The ideal is a Service bar with one bartender attending the server's needs on the floor while the other bartender takes care of customers sitting at the Front bar. On busy nights like Friday and Saturday, staff should be increased evenly at the Service bar and the Front bar, keeping in mind the public relations requirements of the Front bar.

Bartending: Responsible Serving

Patrons drinking responsibly is a bartender's perfect world. However, since alcohol is a drug, some people can't or won't drink with caution. Therefore, it is left to the bartender to be the responsible distributor of the good time.

People skills are essential because more often than not, a person who has become drunk doesn't recognize they are intoxicated. It is best to stop serving someone before they imbibe too much.

There are some obvious behavioral cues that people exhibit:

Inhibitions change along with mannerisms. A talkative person becomes quiet and withdrawn or the opposite; a person becomes overly talkative. Loud behavior, loss of self-control, mood swings are signs a patron has reached their limit.

Inappropriate behavior, using excessively foul language, being aggressive or overly friendly are also cues the person drinking is losing control of their good judgement.

MOONSHINE PINK LEMONADE
2 oz Midnight Moonshine
6 - 7 oz Lemonade
Splash Ocean Spray Cranberry Juice
Catdaddy's relative from Piedmont Distillers, Midnight Moonshine, is the base for this thirst devastating summer drink.

More obvious behavioral cues are lighting one cigarette after another, forgetting things, dropping items, slurred speech and losing train of thought. Coordination becomes a problem. The bartender has to evaluate if another drink should be served if these signs of intoxication appear.

Blood Alcohol Content (BAC) is the legal measurement of the amount of alcohol in a person's blood. It is the gage most governments use when deciding legal limits of alcohol that can be in one's system before being prohibited from operating machinery.

The more alcohol consumed by an individual, the higher the BAC. BAC can be different each time a person drinks. A tolerance to alcohol has no impact on BAC. Time is the only thing that can lower a person's BAC, not coffee, water or soda. It is always a good idea for a person to drink a glass of water between each drink, because alcohol is a diuretic. Food also helps as alcohol is absorbed slower while eating.

It is also important to acknowledge factors that can be catalysts for intoxication. Size, gender, rate of consumption, strength of drink, drug use and food consumed are all factors that effect how quickly a person can become intoxicated.

Smaller people are sometimes affected rapidly by alcohol. Women generally have more body fat than men and reach a higher BAC faster. Drinking shots or gulping drinks, coupled with the strength of the drinks, contribute to how fast a patron may become intoxicated. Drug use, legal or illegal, can also lead to effects that intensify intoxication, depending on the drug in question.

Different countries have different rules concerning the consumption of alcohol, but in any bar, no matter where it is, a good bartender will use a delicate balance of diplomacy, discipline and hawkish observation skills to maintain order, do their best to keep people safe, and whenever possible, avoid problems before they arise. A clear policy is a must, as well as a good sound battle plan for bar staff to deal with the situation, whether it arises or not.

THE WELL

The key element in both the Service bar and the Front bar is the well. The bar's well contains the bottles of spirits used to make the majority of drinks. The well is fairly standard:

Vodka, Gin, Rum, Tequila and one or two types of Whiskey along with White and Sweet Vermouth makes-up the standard well. Many bars also include Triple Sec liqueur and any other spirit that sells exceptionally well. The majority of drinks are made with the well products and a good understanding of the basics of these unique spirits is necessary for purchasing.

The Vodka

Vodka is a white spirit that originated in the 14th century in either Russia or Poland. Vodka has always been distilled from the most plentiful produce available. It can be made from potatoes, but now it is usually various grains. Because it is distilled to a very high proof, it has little flavor. Premium vodkas are distilled three to five times. Vodka does not have to be aged because it is a finished product after distillation. Vodka producers use vegetable charcoal to filter the distilled product. Some credit vodka for starting the cocktail revolution. In the late 1930's Smirnoff Vodka and a restaurant in Los Angeles named the "Cock and Bull" created the "Moscow Mule". This drink became famous and Vodka sales jumped. So did mixed drinks in general.

**The Church is near
But the road is icy.
The Bar is far away
But I will walk carefully.**

- Russian Proverb

DUTCH BERRY
1 1/2 - 2 oz Van Gogh Acai Blueberry Vodka
3 oz Ocean Spray Cranberry Juice
3 oz Grape Juice
1 oz Sour Mix
Splash Soda
In our humble opinion, Van Gogh makes
the best flavored vodkas.

JACKELOPE & TONIC
1 1/2 - 2 oz Jackelope Gin
6 - 7 oz Tonic Water

Jackelope Gin from Peach Street Distillers is a gin smooth enough to drink on the rocks, but strong enough to keep its herbal flavor when mixed with tonic.

TEQUILA GIMLET
2 oz of Grillos Tequila
2 - 3 oz of Lime Cordial
Garnish with Lime

A Tequila Gimlet is easier to make than a Margarita, not as sweet, but still delicious. Grillos Tequila has been our favorite to use with this drink.

The Gin

During Prohibition in America, Gin was made illegal in the U.S. However, it became one of the most popular spirits found at speakeasies. The quality of the Gin available at this time was so bad it was known as bathtub gin, and was often mixed just to make it palatable. American popular culture made Gin an icon through movies and pulp fiction novels.

> **I'm tired of gin,**
> **I'm tired of sin,**
> **And after last night,**
> **Oh boy, am I tired.**
>
> *- Anonymous*

The Tequila

True Tequila can only come from Mexico and production is tightly controlled by the Mexican government. Only five special regions may produce Tequila: Jalisco, Nayarit, Michoacan, Guanajuato and Tamaulipas. Most of the Tequila production occurs in the Jalisco region where the town of Tequila is located. According to Mexican law, all Tequila must be made from harvested agave heart and it must be distilled twice. It's only considered Tequila after the second distillation. At this point, the process varies depending on the type of Tequila being made. Premium Tequila is usually 40 proof. Bulk Tequila is distilled to 55 proof and later diluted with purified water. Most bars use Bulk Tequila in their well.

During distillation Tequila is a white spirit until it is aged in a barrel. This provides the color. Tequila aged at least 60 days is called Reposado, which means Rested. Tequila aged at least one year is called Anejo, which means Aged. White Tequila is known as Blanco but can also be Gold, but this is from color additives. Blanco is usually served chilled on ice for sipping. There is never a worm in a genuine bottle of Tequila. Worms are found in Mezcal, a different type of product made from the agave plant.

The Rum

The production of Rum begins with harvesting sugarcane. The freshly cut cane is milled into a thick dark syrup. From this product comes distilled molasses, which is called Rum. Rum can be clear, golden or dark. Dark Rums have been aged five to seven years. Golden Rum is a blend of aged Rums. Light Rum is popular in nations throughout the Caribbean and the most common Rum used in a bar's well. Many tropical cocktails use Rum because of how well it compliments fruit juice.

The Whiskey

A well Whiskey can be American, Canadian, Irish or Scottish. Price and location are the chief considerations. For example, Jameson's Irish Whiskey is expensive in the U.S. so it might not make a good well Whiskey, but in Asia it's usually priced low enough be in the well. All Whiskies are distilled from grain, but tastes vary.

"Whisky, drink divine,
Why should drivellers bore us
With the praise of wine
When we have thee before us?"

- Toast by Joseph O' Leary,
19th Century Irish Writer

TATTOO TROPIC
1 1/2 - 2 oz Captain Morgan's Tattoo Rum
3 - 4 oz Pineapple Juice
3 - 4 oz Orange Juice
Key to this cocktail is Captain Morgan's Tattoo Rum. This rum is delicious and can easily be enjoyed on the rocks.

The Triple Sec

Triple Sec is made principally from imported orange peel, wild Curacao orange and sweet, aromatic Spanish Valencià orange. This sweet liqueur goes through three distillations. It is a main ingredient in daiquiris, margaritas and many other popular drinks. Because so many drinks call for Triple Sec it should be in the well. Cointreau is a premium brand Triple Sec and recipes often call for it specifically. Some refer to Cointreau as a different product all together.

The Mixers

Mixers are additives that help sell spirits. Juice, soda, aperitifs, cordials, and water allow the bartender to create a variety of flavors, consistencies and colors. The fresher the products, the better the cocktail. Ocean Spray products are extremely consistent in taste and quality. Ocean Spray is also available almost anywhere in the world making it a main-stay mixer for high-end bars and the common denominator at posh cocktail parties.

RED APPLE
1 1/2 - 2 oz Apelkorn
6 - 7 oz Ocean Spray Cranberry Juice
A sweet apple product from Beretzen that seems made to be mixed with Ocean Spray Classic.

The Vermouth

Vermouth's name comes from the German word for wormwood, but was first distilled in Italy. Around 1800 the production of Dry Vermouth, often called White Vermouth, was moved to France where to this day it is called French Vermouth. Sweet Vermouth, or Red Vermouth production stayed in Italy. Both Vermouths are kept in the well for cocktails. Dry Vermouth is used in Martinis while Sweet Vermouth is used in many whiskey cocktails like the Manhattan.

The Syrups

Quality of syrups and a large variety are key to making drinks taste great. Monin has always led the way in terms of both. Internationally acclaimed and with a production history of over 100 years, everyone in the industry knows Monin is the staple for professionals across the planet.

Energy Drinks

A recent trend in bars is the mixing of Energy Drinks with spirits and liqueurs. The carbonation and simple sugar give the drink a boost in flavor and the caffeine and taurine boost energy levels. The most popular is Red Bull, and while a lot of competitors have entered the market in the last ten years, Red Bull has dominated because of its consistency, availability and the fact that it really tastes good with several types of spirits, the most common, vodka and Jagermiester. It was originally introduced in Austria before becoming wildly popular in Asia. It has only really established itself in Western markets over the last five years but it's been so successful that it is known and asked for from coast to coast.

"One Tequila, Two Tequila, Three Tequila, Floor."

- George Carlin,
20th Century Entertainer

TANNED MEXICANO
1 1/2 oz 1921 Cream Tequila
1 1/2 oz 1921 Aged Tequila
1921 Tequila Creme is almost too good. Put it on ice or neat the taste is addictive. It's not overly sweet, but to make it less so, we have added 1921 Anejo to make what we call a Tanned Mexicano.

PRODUCT FOCUS

Although the well spirits are key to all bar operations there are literally hundreds of different spirits out there. Depending on what is popular in the region, whether it be Arak in Indonesia or Japanese Sake, requests from patrons can vary widely. Although your bar might not carry every product under the sun, it's a good idea to at least know what's out there.

See the Taste Glossary for the Flavor, Type, Color and Source of a vast array of the different spirits that may not be available in your region.

The following section discusses three products that beg further description. Whiskey, with its thousands of brands and bottles, is an entity onto itself, and the subject of many books. We'll go into detail about its production and the various locations around the world that make their own unique kinds of this storied liquor.

Absinthe is not new but perhaps requires a proper re-introduction after so many years off the market. Once the drink of choice for artists, writers and most of France, Absinthe was banned in most European countries except for Spain, Portugal and the Czech Repulic, formerly Czechoslovakia. Since Absinthe is currently enjoying a renaissance, even in the United States, we do our part to dispel the myths and get to the bottom of this mysterious spirit.

Bai Jiu is as old as Chinese civilization itself, and it still represents 80% of what Chinese consumers drink. Just as varied and individually unique as Japanese Sake, we'll take a quick look at a few of the more popular brands, there ingredients, and their alcohol content.

> **Moonlight steeped in spring rain,**
> **Blossoms of wisdom -**
> **All from one little cup.**
>
> *- Li Po, 8th Century Chinese Poet*

THE WHISKEY

Whisky or whiskey, which one is the correct spelling? Both are. Of the four notable whiskey producing countries, Ireland and the United States spell the word "whiskey" with the "e" while Scotland and Canada spell it "whisky". The term whiskey comes from the Gaelic usque baugh which means water of life. Later, a slang word usky took over and the English word whiskey evolved. So that's the good word. Now we delve a little deeper into the product itself.

Whiskey Production

Whiskey's main ingredients are grain, water and yeast - it's easy to see why this was originally a farmer's specialty. The differences between whiskies rests primarily amongst the many variables that can effect the product along this very old production process. Each one of these stages can dramatically effect the end result: method of distillation, type of wood used for aging, size of the barrel, and the length of time the barrel is aged. The water source plays a role in quality but the most important factors are the strain of yeast and the type and proportions of grain used. There is a generic 5-step process that is the blueprint for whiskies worldwide.

During malting the grains are cooked. Mashing churns them into a grainy liquid for fermentation, and fermentation is where the yeast is introduced. Yeasts are all unique and companies consider their strains to be guarded company assets. Distillation establishes the alcohol content and we are left with the finished potable spirit. Also known as maturation, the aging of the whiskey gives each one a distinctive color and flavor.

Scotch

Throughout the world, Scotch is often what is served when ordering whisky. Scotch whisky is peaty and a bit stronger tasting than its many cousins. There are several flavors to be aware of when drinking Scotch. There is Single Cask (or Barrel), which is only from that barrel. Single Malt usually contains whisky from several casks from the same batch from the same distillery. Blended Scotch is a combination of different Scotch whiskies, not necessarily from the same distillery. Chivas, Dewars, Ballantine's, Jonnie Walker, Pinch and J & B are just a few blended Scotches. The better blends are light and easy to mix with other ingredients. Single Malts are usually enjoyed neat or with ice, but seldom mixed with any other ingredient.

The Canadian Whiskies

Let's talk about Canadian whiskies. Canadian whiskies like Canadian Club, Crown Royal, Black Velvet, and Canadian Mist are sometimes called "Ryes" because of the misconception that they are made only with rye grain. Actually, the dominant cereal is corn. Most find Canadian whiskeys much smoother, milder, mellower and slightly sweeter than their American counterparts. They are often judged as more flavorful the longer they are aged so Canadian Club 12-year-old is a favorite. Crown Royal has hints of both vanilla and cherry and is so sweet it can be enjoyed straight-up. Although these whiskies aren't all rye, ordering rye and ginger ale will usually get you a Canadian whiskey. Genuine rye whisky is made with at least 51% rye grain and people who drink Canadian Whiskeys might be surprised at the strong flavor and full body of a true rye whiskey.

Irish Whiskey

Irish whiskey dates into antiquity. For centuries Irish whiskey enjoyed an excellent reputation in the world as a better tasting spirit than Scotch. When Scottish farmers started to blend their whiskeys in the mid-nineteenth century the end result was a smoother and more refined product. Irish whiskey dropped-off in popularity.

Today, Irish whiskey is still in the process of making a comeback. It could be because the taste is lighter than Scotch or the fact that it's triple distilled and distillers don't use peat for fire. The peat lends Scotch some of its smoky flavor. The multiple distilling process gives whiskey its own kind soft finish although it still has the complex whiskey taste. By law, whiskey must be aged in a wooden vessel for a minimum of three years. Most are aged much longer.

Almost all of the Irish whiskey distilleries are centered in Cork or Dublin. The major exception is Bushmills, which is located in Northern Ireland in Antrim County. Other notable brands include, John Power, Murphy's, Paddy, Dunphy's, Tullamore Dew and the most global, Jameson's Irish Whiskey.

Bourbon Whiskey

Bourbon whiskey has been in existence since the late 1700's. American Bourbon whiskey gets its name from the county in Kentucky where it was first made. The creation myth behind Bourbon begins in 1789. Elijah Craig, a Baptist Minister, aged some corn whiskey in a wooden barrel that had been charred with fire. The whiskey was acclaimed to be smoother and mellower than previously produced by traditional methods.

MACALLAN ON THE ROCKS
3 oz Macallan Scotch
Ice
It also tastes great with a splash of water. The quality of Macallan products can't be denied.

Conventionally, whiskies were named after the town or city that first distilled them but Reverend Craig lived in Georgetown, Kentucky. With the American Revolution still fresh in the minds of many, a wise marketing decision was made to name it after the county - Bourbon. The county was named Bourbon in honor of the kings of France who had helped America shake-off the shackles of British colonial rule. The plentiful limestone springs, the distinctive red color and the name helped Kentucky Bourbon whiskey compete in the first major market down river: New Orleans.

Farmers distilling whiskey for cash crops could take the equivalent of two-dozen bushels of grain to market in distilled form – in two kegs. Farmers who did not distill could only physically fit two bushels of unprocessed rye, corn, or wheat grain on a wagon. Necessity dictated that distilling spirits become an important part of farming at the time. George Washington himself generated significant retirement revenue from whiskey and his estate distillery is still in operation.

Bourbon whiskey is special. An American Federal Law designates Bourbon as the national spirit of the United States. It must be made from a grain formula of 51% corn and aged in newly charred barrels. In comparison, Tennessee whiskeys use the same constituents but are filtered through charcoal to give them a distinctive flavor. Jack Daniel's is the most famous Tennessee whiskey and because of the filtration process it is not considered Bourbon.

BEAM & CREAM
2 oz favorite Jim Beam small batch bourbon
6 - 7 oz Cream Soda
In the Old American West, Sarsaparilla Soda was found at all soda fountains. It was found in most bars, too.

Production Steps:

1. Malt
2. Mash
3. Ferment
4. Distill
5. Mature

THE ABSINTH

It's not in most wells but it sure used to be. According to the absinth creation myth, it was first distilled in Switzerland 200 years-ago by Pierre Ordinaire, a French doctor who had left France because of the revolution. The recipe was later acquired by Henri-Louis Pernod in 1797. In the mid-nineteenth century absinth started to catch-on after French soldiers stationed overseas began using it to sterilize their water canteens. Word of its potency carried and it became the drink of choice for many of the elite in France's cafe society. The industry-wide grape blight of the 1860's, phylloxera, crippled the European wine industry and absinth filled the void.

There are many classic cocktails that call for absinth but it was often just diluted and sweetened with sugar and water to drink without mixing. The process of sweetening absinth evolved into a number of unique rituals. The steps for one of the more common rituals is as follows:

About three ounces of absinth are poured into a special cocktail glass called the Absinth Drip. An ornate, perforated spoon is then set on the rim of the glass and a sugar cube is placed on top. Water is dripped onto the sugar to melt it into the waiting liquid below. How much water depends on the taste of the one drinking but the ratio

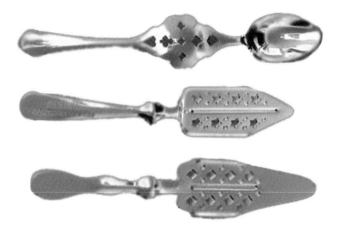

should be somewhere between 5:1 to 3:1. As the water fills the glass, real absinth changes color from an olive green to an opaque, milky, green-white. This is called the louche [verb]. An absinth louches well if the fluid becomes opaque.

At the peak of its popularity in 1913 France consumed 10.5 million gallons of absinth. In 1915 France banned absinth. The only European countries not to ban absinth were Spain, Portugal and Czechoslovakia. Interestingly enough, no major crime waves have been attributed to absinth in those countries over the past one hundred years.

Today the European Union allows the sale of absinth, limiting it to 10 milligrams of thujone-per-kilogram. Thujone is the active ingredient in absinth. The alcohol in absinth is more of a delivery vehicle for the herbs than anything else. Different absinth brands use different amounts of specific herbs which affect the taste as well as the experience. They play-off of each other in a synergistic way and authentic absinth recipes are closely-guarded industrial secrets. Each brand claims a different experience depending on the herbs. The desired effect has been described as a "clear-headed inebriation".

Thanks to the Internet, absinth is available almost anywhere as long as it is used for personal consumption. However, there are still a lot of counterfeit brands claiming to be absinth and the real thing is hard to find. Confusing things further is the current state of the absinth ban. As of 2008 many countries have lifted their respective bans on absinth while a few stubborn ones continue to sit-on-the-fence.

THE BAI JIU

Bai jiu is as ancient as Chinese culture itself. Dating back to the Neolithic Age, bai jiu, pronounced *bye joe* in English, accounts for roughly 80% of all the spirits consumed in China today. It is a staple of weddings and all manner of gatherings that call for spirits. While some people claim the aroma is the key to a good bai jiu, still others enjoy bai jiu with little or no aroma. Below are just a few of the many different kinds:

Fen jiu - Dates back to the Northern and Southern Dynasties (550 A.D.). It is the original Chinese white spirit made from sorghum.

Alcohol content by volume: 16%

Zhu Ye Qing jiu - Brewed with select Chinese herbal medicine. One of the ingredients is bamboo leaves which gives it a greenish color and its name.

Alcohol content by volume: 18%

Mao Tai jiu - A production history of over 200 years. From Mao Tai town in Guizhou Province, it is made from wheat and sorghum with a unique seven-cycle distilling process. This spirit was made famous in the Western world when the Chinese government served it during various state banquets that entertained U.S. presidents.

Alcohol content by volume: 55-57%

Gao Liang jiu - Goa Liang is the Chinese name for sorghum. Besides sorghum, the brewing process also uses barley and wheat. It originates from Da Zhi Gu during the Ming Dynasty. Today, Taiwan is the largest producer of gao liang jiu.

Alcohol content by volume: 32% or 38-39%

Mei Gui Lu jiu (Rose Essence Spirit) - Gao liang jiu distilled from a special species of rose and crystal sugar.

Alcohol content by volume: 52%

Wu Jia Pi jiu - A variety of gao liang jiu with a unique selection of Chinese herbal medicines added to the brew.

Alcohol content by volume: 54-55%

Da Gu jiu - Originated in Sichuan Province over 300 years ago. This spirit is made of sorghum and wheat and involves a unique aging process.

Alcohol content by volume: 54-55%

Bidding Farewell

Passion so deep appears as none;
Before these farewell cups, unable even to smile.
The candle too takes pity on our parting,
Shedding tears until the coming of dawn.

- Du Mu, 9th Century Chinese Poet

Sheung Jing jiu and San Jing jiu - Special Double Distilled and Triple Distilled Spirits.

Alcohol content by volume: 61-63%

San Hua jiu (Three Flowers Spirit) - A rice spirit with an allegedly thousand-year-old history. It is famous for the fragrant herbs added and the use of spring water from Mount Elephant in the Guilin region.

Alcohol content by volume: 55%

Fujian Glutinous Rice Spirit - Made by adding a long list of expensive Chinese herbal medicines, glutinous rice and a distilled, low-alcohol rice spirit. The unique brewing technique involves rectifying with a different kind of spirit. It has a reddish-orange color.

Alcohol content by volume: 46%

Hua Diao jiu - A variety of Yellow Spirit originating from Shaoxing, Zhejiang. It is made from glutinous rice and wheat.

Alcohol content by volume: 63-65%

For the moment, Drinking Wine

Cen, dear sir, and Brother Dan Qui-
For the moment drink, and don't put down your cups.
Just lend your ears to the song I have to sing;
Bells and drums and costly foods count for nothing;
All that matters is never sobering up!
Saints and sages through the ages are now forgot,
Save those who lingered in their cups.
When Prince Chen feasted in the Peace and Pleasure Hall,
He served precious wine for the delight of everyone.
How can a good host ever stint for a drink?
Straightaway I'll buy enough for all.
Thoroughbreds and costly furs?
Let's call my son to pawn them for the best wine.
Together we shall banish the most endless, ancient sorrow.

- Li Bai, 8th Century Chinese Poet

An ultra premium bai jiu that boasts a production history of over 600 years.

INFUSIONS

Maceration

The basic principal of infusions is the marrying of a choice flavor with a chosen spirit to create a new product. This is a great way to experiment with personal tastes. The general public has largely accepted infused vodkas, rums and gins. These new flavors allow a bartender an almost unlimited *palette* from which to appeal to the a patron's *palate*. Using a technique called maceration, and an innate sense of adventure, we can create our own marvelous infusions. Maceration is a time-tested process that is similar to steeping tea, as it adds both flavor and color, increasing the complexity of any spirit.

Liquor companies use artificial flavoring agents to simulate maceration when mass-producing bottles of citron vodka, spiced rum and cherry brandy. To make authentic infusions we need only follow the proper protocol, which is fairly simple.

Put the desired ingredients (fruits, nuts, herbs, or spices) in a dark glass vessel with the chosen spirit and cover it with a lid, but not air-tight. Be sure to allow for the Angel's Share - the spirit lost to evaporation - that also happens when spirits are aged in wooden barrels. Place out of direct light. Age to taste.

> "It has long been recognized that the problems with alcohol relate not to the use of a bad thing, but to the abuse of a good thing."
>
> *- Abraham Lincoln*
> *19th Century American President*

In order to demonstrate the versatility of maceration, we've applied it to two unique products, absinth and bai jiu, with excellent results. The following notes are a guideline to ideal outcomes, but like inventing new drinks, creating your own infusions just requires a little imagination and product knowledge.

LIME

BANANA

Lime Bai Jiu Infusion

Ingredients
- 3 oz of bai jiu
- 1 lime quartered with one wedge chopped

Day 2:
AROMA: Takes on a mild citrus smell.
BAI JIU BITE: Becomes less pronounced.

Day 5:
AROMA: Slightly more lime essence.
BAI JIU BITE: Very little left.

Day 7:
AROMA: Developed citrus smell.
BAI JIU BITE: There is no trace of bai jiu aroma.

Day 14:
AROMA: Smell is now completely like lime.
COLOR: Has become light yellow.
TASTE: Has a strong citrus flavor with a hint of peel.
BAI JIU BITE: The bite is gone.

Day 22:
AROMA: A fine lime liquor.
COLOR: Light yellow.
TASTE: Has become a little bit bitter from the peel but still mellower than a citron vodka or gin.

NOTES: Optimum maceration time 12 - 15 days.

Lime Bai Jiu and Tonic- 1 1/2 oz of bai jiu macerated with lime, 5 - 6 of tonic. Pour over ice in a 12 oz Collins glass and stir. Garnish with a lime.

Banana Bai Jiu Infusion

Ingredients
- 3 oz of bai jiu
- 1/2 banana sliced into pieces

Day 2:
AROMA: Smell of Banana is there.
BAI JIU BITE: Still strong.

Day 5:
AROMA: Banana has almost neutralized bai jiu.
BAI JIU BITE: Slight.

Day 7:
AROMA: Smell unchanged. Banana is dominant.
BAI JIU BITE: Slight.

Day 14:
AROMA: Smell of banana and slight vanilla.
COLOR: Light yellow with slight cloudiness. TASTE: Sweet and strongly banana. Delicious.
BAI JIU BITE: None.

Day 22:
AROMA: Strong banana with vanilla and spice.
COLOR: Slightly cloudy and light yellow.
TASTE: Excellent flavor. A sipping bai jiu.
BAI JIU BITE: None.

NOTES: Optimum maceration time 14 - 21 days.

Banana Bai Jiu Cocktail- 1 1/2 oz of bai jiu macerated with banana, 2 oz of TGI Friday's Colada mix, 2 oz milk. Shake and serve in a Whiskey glass.

STRAWBERRY GRAPE

Strawberry Bai Jiu Infusion

Ingredients
- 3 oz of bai jiu
- 3 strawberries sliced

Day 6:
AROMA: Strawberry smell is strong.
BAI JIU BITE: Soft.

Day 8:
AROMA: Smell is similar to strawberry jam.
COLOR: Light red.
TASTE: Strawberry but bai jiu still recognizable.
BAI JIU BITE: Medium.

Day 13:
AROMA: Strong strawberry, slight bai jiu.
COLOR: Pinkish red.
TASTE: Strong strawberry, but not sweet.
BAI JIU BITE: Much softer.

Day 24:
AROMA: Bai jiu present, strawberry dominates.
COLOR: Pink red.
TASTE: Bai jiu hints with strawberry. Not sweet.

NOTES: Optimum maceration time 8 - 31 days.

Strawberry Bai Jiu Cocktail: Build in a Collins glass. 1 1/2 oz bai jiu macerated with strawberry, 1 oz sweet and sour, 4- 5 oz of orange juice. Shake and serve.

Grape Absinth Infusion

Ingredients
- 8 seedless black grapes split into halves
- 2.5 oz of Oliva Absinth

Day 5:
AROMA: Lighter smell of absinth. No grape.
COLOR: Pink, clear

Day 10:
AROMA: Absinth, but softer.
COLOR: Light pink/purple, clear.
TASTE: A little sweet. Very little absinth bite. Grape flavor comes through. Almost sipping quality.

Day 22:
AROMA: Light absinth smell.
COLOR: Light pink, sapphire, clear.
TASTE: Sweet with a little bitter after taste. Even better than on Day 10.

Day 34:
AROMA: Soft absinth smell. Slight grape essence.
COLOR: Light pink, clear.
TASTE: Sweet, grape taste with a little absinth bite.

NOTES: Optimum maceration time 3-4 weeks.

Infused Grape Absinth With Water: 1 part absinth macerated with grape, 4 parts water. Serve in a Whiskey glass. Takes on a cloudy purple hue. There is a slight smell of Absinth. Taste is very smooth a little sweet.

APPLE

PEACH

Apple Absinth Infusion

Ingredients
- 1/8 of Red Delicious apple sliced into 4-5 pieces and halve again making 8 - 10 wedges
- 2.5 oz of Oliva Absinth

Day 5:
AROMA: Strong absinth with traces of apple.
COLOR: Gold, clear.

Day 10:
AROMA: Light absinth with light apple scent.
COLOR: Gold, clear.
TASTE: Absinth flavor is soft. Slightly sweet apple flavor.

Day 22:
AROMA: Light apple, absinth is very light.
COLOR: Gold like apple juice, clear.
TASTE: Absinth is soft. Apple is getting stronger.

Day 34:
AROMA: Light apple, absinth very light.
COLOR: Gold, clear.
TASTE: Strong apple. A little sweet. Absinth still has a bite, but very soft.

NOTES: Optimum maceration time 3 - 4 weeks.

Infused Apple Absinth With Water: 1 part absinth macerated with apple, 4 parts water. Serve in a Whiskey glass. Takes on a cloudy golden hue. Apple taste is dominant, but there is still a flavor of herbal Absinth. The anis taste is now very light.

Peach Absinth Infusion

Ingredients
- 1/4 peach cut up into slices
- 2.5 oz of Oliva Absinth

Day 5:
AROMA: Strong smell of absinth, hint of peach.
COLOR: Brownish gold, clear.

Day 10:
AROMA: Light absinth with light peach scent.
COLOR: Pale gold, clear.
TASTE: A little sweet. Peach flavor with absinth bite after-taste. Smooth.

Day 22:
AROMA: Peach scent, light absinth smell.
COLOR: Gold, clear.
TASTE: Light peach flavor with a little bitter aftertaste.

Day 34:
COLOR: Gold and yellow. Clear.
AROMA: Light peach scent, light absinth smell.
TASTE: Peach flavor, a little sweet, absinth herbs present. Could sip, very smooth.

NOTES: Optimum maceration time 3 - 4 weeks.

Infused Peach Absinth With Water: 1 part absinth macerated with peach, 4 parts water. Serve in a Whiskey glass. Very smooth with a pleasant peach scent. Water tones down both flavors but peach is still present.

MATH

Beyond the Recipe Books

A bar operation has math running through it because this is a liquid business. The bartender has to know the pour cost per bottle and monitor the cycle that a bottle goes through from when it's opened to the recycle bin.

An operating bartender has to set ordering priorities, handle purchases, set-up a bar inventory system, and have a register account for money in a way that satisfies the owner. For those who love math, this is a dream-job.

Bottles sitting behind the bar, and especially the ones in the well, represent money. Some make for attractive decoration, but if they sit on a shelf for six months, they are not a priority brand. Or are they? A bottle that sits and gets little attention is a bottle that is not being properly promoted by the bar. Because it is potential revenue, it is not good enough to let it sit there until someone orders it. Be proactive and move it in a promotion.

A bottle will always move faster when it's an ingredient in a hot drink special. This is a chance for a bar to turn slow sellers into a real opportunity. When a bar can sell a slow-moving spirit the company that owns the brand will usually offer-up discounts or free promotional tools. With creative drink promotions there are no slow-sellers. However, the well is where dependable revenue is generated.

The well contains the bottles used as a base in most cocktails. The well is rum, vodka, gin, tequila, scotch, whiskey, triple sec, dry vermouth and sweet vermouth, depending on what kind of drinks are popular in that bar. The well moves the most volume, so it is every spirit company's dream to get their brands into a bar's well.

Whatever the brands selected, an owners should know what their pour cost is for each well bottle. Other bottles are important, but this is the area to get the pour cost down. Negotiating deals with distributors or brand marketing teams can fetch lower pour costs, or you can select the most economical spirit in each category.

Mike's money is on working with the marketing team of a spirit company strategically because they will usually help promote a bar alongside their brand, but only if the math makes sense.

TABLES

STANDARD BOTTLE QUANTITY

Bottle Size	Fluid Ounces	Bottles Per Case	Liters Per Case	Gallons Per Case
4 Liter	135	N/A	N/A	N/A
3 Liter	101	4	12	3.2
1.75 Liter	59	6	10.5	2.8
1.5 Liter	50.7	6	9	2.3
1 Liter	33	12	12	3.1
750 ml	25	12	9	2.3
500 ml	16.9	24	12	3.2
375 ml	12.7	24	9	2.4
200 ml	6.8	48	9.6	2.5
187 ml	6.3	48	9	2.4
100 ml	3.4	60	6	1.6
50 ml	1.7	120	6	1.6

DRINKS PER BOTTLE

Serving Size	750 ml Bottle	1 Liter Bottle	1.75 Liter Bottle
1 ounce	25	33	59
1 1/4 ounce	20	27	47
1 1/2 ounce	17	22	39
2 ounce	13	17	30

There are 25 shots (30 ml - 1 oz) in a 750 ml bottle. The bottle price dictates the pour cost. If a bottle costs $10, then 10 ÷ 25 means a pour cost of 40 cents. This is where a bar can negotiate. Distributors often offer promotional parties or extra-stock deals to make the sale, but knowing the exact pour cost of competing products gives the buyer real power to decide their course of action, whatever the sales incentives may be.

STANDARD BAR MEASUREMENTS

Bar Measurement	Metric Equivalent	Standard Equivalent
1 Dash	0.9 ml	1/32 ounce
1 Teaspoon	3.7 ml	1/8 ounce
1 Tablespoon	11.1 ml	3/8 ounce
1 Pony	29.5 ml	1 ounce
1 Jigger	44.5 ml	1.5 ounces
1 Miniature	59.2 ml	2 ounces
1 Wine Glass	119 ml	4 ounces
1 Split	177 ml	6 ounces
1 Half Pint	257 ml	8 ounces
1 Tenth	378.9 ml	12.8 ounces
1 Pint	472 ml	16 ounces
1 Fifth	755.2 ml	25.6 ounces
1 Quart	944 ml	32 ounces
1 Imperial Quart	1.14 Liters	38.4 ounces
1 Magnum	1.5 Liters	52 ounces
1 Half Gallon	1.9 Liters	64 ounces
1 Gallon	3.8 Liters	128 ounces

CALORIE COUNTS

Type of Spirit	Calories Per Serving
Champagne	23
Wine (24 proof)	23
Liqueurs (34-48 proof)	86 -105
Straight Spirits	78
80 proof	65
86 proof	70
90 proof	74
150 proof	138

PROFIT

If you're running a business, you have to generate revenue, whatever you hand over the bar. Once you accept this basic principle, the question becomes "What's the bottom line?" If you don't know then chances are you're leaking money. Determining the pour cost for each bottle gives you an accurate Beverage Cost. This can be used to calculate Profit Margin to set a logical Sales Price.

FULL MOON MARTINI

Ingredients	Proportion	Cost	(USD)
Grand Marnier	1 oz	$1.00	
Amaretto	1.2 oz	$ .27	
Orange Juice	3 oz	$ .20	
Full Moon Martini		Beverage Cost = $1.47	

Sales Price	$5.60
Subtract Beverage Cost	- $1.47
Gross Profit	$4.13
Gross Profit ÷ Sales Price **X 100**	Profit = 73.75%

Although the cost of the drink is always the same, adjusting the Sales Price by sixty cents increases the Profit Margin by 2.54%

Sales Price	$6.20
Subtract Beverage Cost	- $1.47
Gross Profit	$4.73
Gross Profit ÷ Sales Price **X 100**	Profit = 76.29%

*Besides setting the basic Sales Price this formula is useful for planning for expected revenue, managing stock and running drink promotions.

**The cocktail is a pleasant drink,
It's mild and harmless, I don't think!
When you've had one, you call for two,
And then you don't care what you do!
At four I sought my whirling bed,
At eight I woke with such a head -
It is no time for mirth or laughter -
The cold grey dawn of the morning after!**

*- George Ade,
Late 19th Century American Writer*

PERIPHERALS

Just in case you were thinking about opening up a bar, or just wanted to have a really well-stocked bar for your house parties, here are some things you're going to need in order to have the best bar on the block.

EQUIPMENT ESSENTIALS

Equipment Item	Quantity	Cost
Glasses	120	$650.00
Shakers	16	$170.00
Blender	1	$310.00
Ice Crusher	1	$ 15.00
Tea Towel	10	$ 30.00
Bar Tray	3	$ 15.00
Cutting Board	1	$ 9.00
Knives	4	$ 60.00
Rolling Pin	1	$ 9.00
Muddler	2	$ 19.00
Cocktail Stir Spoon	2	$ 9.00
Spouts for Bottles	10	$ 30.00
Shot Measure Glass	2	$ 6.00
Strainers	16	$ 80.00
Total:		$1,412.00

DISPOSABLE ESSENTIALS

Disposable Item	Cost
Assorted Fresh Fruit	$15.00
Cherries	$25.00
Citrus Fruits	$6.00
Sugar Water	$15.00
Lemon Juice	$6.00
Straws	$1.50
Swords	$1.50
Napkins	$1.00
Juices	$90.00
Coffee	$30.00
Spices	$80.00
Bitters	$80.00
Fresh herbs	$15.00
Total:	$366.00

TECHNOLOGY

Just like any other business in today's world the nightclub and bar industry depends on modern technology to stay competitive.

"Boys should abstain from all use of wine until their 18th year, for it is wrong to add fire to fire."

- Plato,
Ancient Philosopher

One hundred years ago, a National Cash Register (NCR) machine was considered cutting-edge technology. It could tally a total as sales were rung-in. At the end of a shift, this made life easier.

For the next sixty years, there wasn't much improvement.

In the late 1970's and early 1980's, a company called Micros came up with a register that had software programs built-in, rudimentary compared with what is available today, but these saved even more time.

There has been no turning back. Technology is now a key element of bar operations and tracking pours, inventory, even learning the spending habits of your customer base are becoming standard components of all bar operating systems.

Bar operating systems are becoming so advanced this textbook would be remiss if it did not acknowledge what is available at this point in time. However, this is an ongoing revolution that is far from complete. This is a brief break-down of what is available today and a look at what will be mainstream in the future.

Technology Keywords
Some basic vocabulary used around the modern register.

POS: Point Of Sale is wherever a transaction takes place

Software: A Program running on a computer

Hardware: Electronic equipment like a computer or Touch Screen Device

Touch Screen Device: Computer hardware allowing users to interface with the computer by way of touching the screen.

An Electronic Point of Sale Terminal (EPOS) is a combination of Hardware/Software that allows a transaction to occur electronically. This may involve cash, debit card, credit card or other payment methods.

Far from simply a computerized cash register, the speed and convenience of EPOS systems has proven itself over the last decade, and with the cost of flat screen and touchscreen technology dropping rapidly, it will soon become the normal way to transact business in bars.

TECHNOLOGY

A good EPOS System for a bar or restaurant should cover these bases:

* Server or cashier banking or a combination of both

* Separate checks at any time in the order cycle

* Send items (Beverages, Appetizers) to be prepared while remaining in the order process

* Match Beverages with Cover counts

* Track Voids, Deletes and No Sales

* Start an order by touching a picture of the table or entering table number

* Configure the layout of your touch screens. Choose the size and color of the "buttons"

* Menus and prices by workstation, day of week and time of day

* Bar terminals that include separate tally for "cash and carry" operations

* Bar tab capabilities that include assigning names and pre-authorizations for credit cards

* "Happy Hour" pricing and menu changes occur automatically

* Interface to video security systems to record items

* Choice of "like item" consolidation in kitchens and bars

* Order routing for items to appear at appropriate prep station

* Expediter printer or video monitor display

* Ability to change routing schemes during the day from any touch screen

These features make the complex bookkeeping methods of past bar systems seem archaic. With customizable interfaces, these programs are designed from the ground-up with bars in mind.

Although inferior software can actually hamper speed and efficiency, a well-designed and properly integrated POS System can dramatically increase transaction times, slicing precious seconds off transactions that add-up to increased sales.

TECHNOLOGY

POS Security

To a POS Terminal bartenders are known as Users. Users can be uniquely identified when they sign-in to register a transaction - either by card swipe, key code or fingerprint, known as biometrics. According to Glenn Grossi, of Future POS, biometrics is already very well established in the industry and the future holds even faster innovations like Proximity Bracelets. These bracelets will allow automatic User sign-in when the hand approaches the touch-screen, and User sign-out when it goes back to making drinks. Future POS's current system allows Users to fully customize all aspects of the interface - it will even verify a driver's license.

Most high-end programs can seamlessly integrate Payroll and Purchasing, if not a whole bar's Book of Accounts into Quickbooks or other business accounting software programs that can exchange data.

There are a large number of players in this industry, despite the obvious leaders - Micros and Simple. A combination Touch Screen Device and customizable Program are not always available from the same company as some of them are strictly hardware providers. However, the larger and more innovative players like Future POS sell their own hardware loaded with their own program with an ever increasing amount of Internet support - Security/Accounting/Price Indexing/Age Verification and Access Control.

For strictly inventory, companies like Accubar and Berg Company use bar code readers and tablet pen technology to integrate individual bottle volumes with an index of thousands of bottle shapes and sizes. This allows a bartender to accurately take stock of the open bottles at the end of the day.

APPLE JACK STONE SOUR
1 1/2 - 2 oz Apple Jack or Laird's Apple Brandy
3 - 4 oz Sour Mix
Splash of Orange Juice
Garnish with orange wheel and cherry

The Northern US is the home of Apple Jack. When colonists first started making spirits, fruit brandies were the most common. Laird's has kept this tradition alive with their different apple brandies. The Apple Jack Stone Sour is one of the best sours and a great way to enjoy a fairly under utilized spirit.

TECHNOLOGY

The Internet

The Internet has allowed large corporate bodies to better account for every last cent and deal with their own set of unique problems like nation-wide discounts on specific items, gift cards and other types of large-scale promotions native to franchises. This same technology is now available to anyone that owns a bar and the price keeps getting lower.

It's a tough industry for these providers because touch screens are just like flat-screen monitors - they are getting cheaper every year. So the real competitors are hooking clients with easy-to-use programs, then fulfilling all the hardware needs for that system at a competitive price. As with all new technology - it's all about the support and the Internet allows engineers - not delivery guys - to crawl inside your POS Terminal from anywhere and see what's wrong.

Customer Interaction

Just as the old cash register has gone the way of the Dodo (NCR now makes ATMs), so has the Jukebox. The next generation of bar and nightclub technology is not yet widely available, but like Apple's iPhone, it just seems like the next logical step. It's called Surface Computing, and what the iPhone did for the cell phone, Surface Computing could do for the patron's table top. Aside from the novelty of being able to interact with your table-top using multi-touch screens, drag-and-drop ordering, just being able to pay by placing a credit card down make this a worthy investment for any upscale urban cocktail lounge. Integrated promotions, music and video selections can all be selected by patrons from the comfort of their seat.

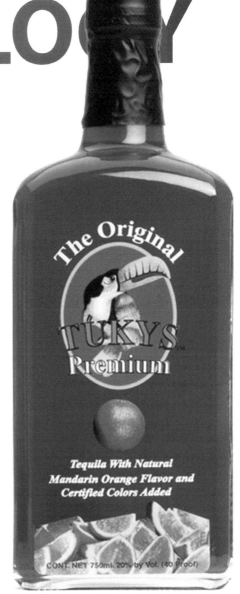

TUKY'S SUNRISE
1 1/2 - 2 oz Tuky's Mandarin Orange Tequila
6 -7 oz Orange Juice
A Tuky's Sunrise is another tequila cocktail that is as easy to make as it is delicious.

Standard Abbreviations

English is the standard when making drinks in large international hotels and restaurant chains. There are some differences from place to place, but the following list is a very efficient ordering system for a busy service bar.

Example: V/T

V = vodka
/ = with
T = tonic.

Well Liquor

Blended Whiskey	= Bl
Bourbon	= B
Brandy	= Br
Gin	= G
Rum	= R
Scotch	= S
Tequila	= T
Vodka	= V

Mixers

Coffee	= Cof
Cola	= C
Cranberry Juice	= Cran
Diet Coke	= Diet
Ginger Ale	= Ginger
Grapefruit Juice	= Grape
Half and Half Or Cream	= Cr
Lemon Juice	= LJ
Orange Juice	= OJ
Pineapple Juice	= PJ
Soda Water Or Seltzer	= S
Seven-Up	= 7
Sweet and Sour	= SS
Tomato Juice	= TJ
Water	= W

Name Brand Spirit

Absolut Vodka	= Abso
Absolut Citron	= Citron
Absolut Peppar	= Peppar
Absolut Kurrant	= Kurrant
Absolut Mandarin	= Mandarin
Abssolut Peach	= Abso Peach
Bacardi Light Rum	= Bac
Bacardi Black Label	= Bac Bl
Bacardi 151	= Bac 151
Beefeater Gin	= Beef
Bombay Gin	= Bom
Bombay Sapphire	= Sapph
Bookers Bourbon	= Bookers
Bushmill's Irish	= Bush
Canadian Club	= CC
Chivas Regal	= Chivas
Chivas Regal Salute	= Salute
Courvoisier VS	= Cou VS
Courvoisier VSOP	= Cou VSOP
Crown Royal	= Crown
Cuervo Gold Tequila	= Gold
Cuervo 1800	= 1800
Dewar's Scotch	= Dewars
Dimple Scotch	= Dimple
E & J Brandy	= EJ
Glenfiddich	= Fiddich
Glenlivet	= Livet
Jameson Irish	= Jameson
Jack Daniels	= Jack
Jim Beam Bourbon	= Beam
Jim Beam Black	= Beam Bl
J. Walker Black	= JW Bl
J. Walker Blue	= JW Blu
J. Walker Red	= JW Red
Makers Mark Bourbon	= Makers
Myer's Rum	= Myers

Sauza Tequila   = Sauza
Smirnoff Vodka   = Smirnoff
Stolichnaya Vodka   = Stoli
Tanqueray Gin   = Tanq
Wild Turkey Bourbon   = Turk

Name Brand Liqueurs

Amaretto di Saronno   = Amo
Bailey's Irish Cream   = Baileys
Benedictine   = Ben
Chambord   = Chambord
Cointreau   = Coin
Drambuie   = Dram
Frangelico   = Fran
Galliano   = Gall
Grand Marnier   = GM or Marnier
Jagermeister   = Jager

*Check out our website for even more practical information for optimizing your bar operations.

Kahlua   = Kah
Midori   = Midori
Ouzo   = Ouzo
Peach Schnapps   = Peach
Peppermint Schnapps = Peppermint
Sambuca   = Sambuca
Southern Comfort   = SoCo or Comort
Tia Maria   = Tia

Pouring Instructions

Back	= Bk	A glass of something with the drink
Double	= Dbl	Twice the amount of alcohol
Dry	= Dry	Very little Vermouth desired
Extra Dry	= Xdry	Almost no Vermouth to be used
Mist	= Mist	Crushed Ice
Neat	= Neat	Drink not chilled in any way
Olive	= Olive	A garnish used mostly in Martinis
Perfect	= Perf	A cocktail with equal parts of Sweet and white Vermouth
Presbyterian	= Press	Drink with mixer equal parts Ginger ale and Soda water
Rocks	= R or X	Ice
Shot	= shot	Shot glass of drink
Splash	= Spl	less than 1/8 of an oz - very little
Straight Up	= Up	Drink with no Ice
Tall	= Tall	A drink put in a tall glass
Twist	= Tw	Rind of citrus rimmed on glass
Virgin	= Virgin	No alcohol in drink

Sample Abbreviated Recipes

Drink Name	Abbreviation	Quick Recipe
Black Russian	Bl Russ	V/ Kahlua
Bloody Maria	Maria	T/ TJ/ Spices
Bloody Mary	Mary	V/ TJ/ Spices
Bocci Ball	Bocci	Amo/ OJ
Brandy Alexander	Alex	Br/ Crème de Cacao/ Cr
Brandy Manhattan	Br/Man	Br/ Sweet vermouth/ bitters
Cape Cod	Cod or V/ Cran	V/ Cran
Colorado Bulldog	Bulldog	V/ Kahlua/ Cr/ C
Cosmopolitan	Cosmo	V/Cran/ Lime Cordial/ Coin
Cuba Libre	Cuba	R/ C/ Lime Wedge
Daiquiri	Daiq	R/ LJ or SS/ Triple Sec
Dry Manhattan	Dry/Man	B/dash Sweet Vermouth/bitters
Dry Martini	Dry/Marti	G/dash White Vermouth
Fuzzy Navel	Fuzzy	Peach / OJ
Gimlet	Gim	G/ Lime cordial
Golden Cadillac	Caddy	White Crème de Cacao/Gall/Cr
Greyhound	Grey or V/Grape	V/ Grape
Harvey Wallbanger	Harvey	Gall/ V / OJ
Irish Coffee	Irish	Coffee/ Jameson
Kamikaze	Kami	V/ Lime Cordial/ Triple Sec
Keoki Coffee	Keoki	Coffee/ Br/ Kahlua

The Sex-On-The-Beach Effect:

There are a few cocktails that have the same name but are really all different. An excellent example of this type of cocktail is Sex on the Beach. Here are some different recipes for the same drink. None are wrong. It's a case of the name becoming more important than the standardized recipe.

- Michael Armstrong

Sex on the Beach in Washington D.C.

Collins or Highball glass
3/4 oz. Midori/ 3/4 oz. Chambord/ 3/4 oz. V/
Fill glass with 1/2 SS and 1/2 PJ

Sex on the Beach in Waikiki, Hawaii.

Tropical Glass
1 oz. SoCo/ 3/4 oz. Chambord/
Fill glass with 1/2 OJ and 1/2 PJ

Sample Abbreviated Recipes

Drink Name	Abbreviation	Quick Recipe
Kir	Kir	Crème de Casis/ White Wine
Long Island Tea	Tea	V/T/G/R/ Triple Sec/ LJ/ C
Manhattan	Man	B/ Sweet Vermouth
Margarita	Marg or Rita	T/ Triple Sec/ LJ/ SS
Martini	Marti	G/ White Vermouth
Old Fashion	OF or Old Fash	B/ Sweet Vermouth
Pina Colada	Pina	R/ Coconut C/ PJ
Presbyterian	Press	Spirit/ S/ 7
Rob Roy	Rob	S/ Sweet Vermouth
Rusty Nail	Nail	S/ Dram
Screwdriver	Screw	V/ OJ
Seabreeze	Breeze	V/ Cran / Grape
Singapore Sling	Sling	G/ Cherry Br/ PJ / LJ
Sombrero	Kah/ Cr	Kah/ Cr
Stinger	Sting	Spirit/White Crème de Menthe
Tequila Sunrise	Sunrise	T/ OJ/ Grenadine
Toasted Almond	T/A	Kah/ Amo/ Cr
Tom Collins	Tom	G/ LJ/ S
Vodka Gimlet	V/Gim	V/ Lime cordial
Vodka Martini	V/ Marti	V/ White Vermouth
Whiskey Sour	Wh/ Sour	Wh/ SS
White Russian	Wh/ Russ	V/ Kah/ Cr

Sex on Beach in Saratoga, Wyoming

Collins or Highball
3/4 oz. V/ 3/4 oz. Chambord/ 3/4 oz. Peach/ Fill 1/2 SS and 1/2 OJ

Sex on the Beach in a few places around the world.

Collins Glass or Highball Glass
3/4 oz. Midori/ 3/4 oz. Chambord/ Fill with PJ

They all taste like Sex on the Beach - and even though these recipes all use Chambord, it's very expensive and some bartenders have been known to substitute a black raspberry liqueur called Crème de Mure. This does change the taste a little, but not much. A good bartender can make a drink taste great – without all the ingredients listed in a book.

RECIPES

What would this book be if it didn't have a decent index of specially chosen classic recipes inside?

Alabama Slammer- Build in a Collins glass with ice. 1 oz of Southern Comfort, 3/4 oz amaretto, 1/4 oz grenadine, 1 oz lime juice, 4-5 oz orange juice. Shake and serve.

Angel's Kiss- 1 1/2 oz of Kahlua, 1 1/2 oz of white creme de cacao, 2-3 oz half/half cream. Chill in a shaker and pour into a Martini glass.

Bamboo Cocktail- 1 1/2 oz Sherry, 3/4 oz dry vermouth, dash bitters, chill with ice, strain, serve in a Martini glass.

Bee's Knees- 2 oz gin, 1/2 oz lime juice, 1 tbsp honey. Put in shaker, chill, pour into a Martini glass. Garnish with a lemon wheel.

Between-the-Sheets- 3/4 oz gin, 3/4 oz white rum, 3/4 oz Cointreau, 3/4 oz lemon juice. Put in shaker, chill, pour into a Martini glass. Garnish with a lemon twist.

Black Russian- Build in a Whiskey glass with ice. 1 1/2 oz vodka, 1 1/2 Kahlua. Stir and serve.

Blue Hawaiian- Build in a Tropical glass with ice. 1 oz coconut rum, 1 oz blue curacao, 5-6 oz pineapple juice. Garnish with a cherry.

MEKHONG WHISKEY & COKE
Mekong Whiskey and Coke,
1 1/2 - 2 oz of Mekong Traditional Whiskey
6 - 7 oz of coke
Garnish with a lime

If you like coke, Mekong Whiskey is the product to mix it with. It goes down smooth and the Thai Beverage spirit keeps it taste. Recently introduced to North America, it has long been a staple at the beach resorts of Thailand.

RECIPES

Bloody Mary- Build in a 10-12 oz Tumbler glass with ice. 1 1/2 oz of vodka, 5-6 oz V8 vegetable juice, 1/2 tbsp worcestershire sauce, 2 dashes Tobasco sauce, 3 dashes celery salt, 3 dashes black pepper, 1/4 tbsp horseradish (optional). Shake ingredients. Garnish with a lime and celery stick.

Bocci Ball- Build in a Collins glass. 1 1/2 oz amaretto, 5 - 6 oz orange juice, 1 tbsp sweet and sour. Garnish with an orange slice.

Boilermaker- Carefully drop a shot glass with 1 1/2 oz whiskey into a 10 oz pint glass of beer.

Brandy Alexander- 1 oz dark creme de cacao, 1 oz brandy/cognac, 2-3 oz Half/Half cream. Put in shaker, chill, pour into a Martini glass.

Bronx- 1 oz gin, 1/2 oz dry vermouth, 1/2 sweet vermouth, 1 oz orange juice, chill in shaker, pour in a Martini glass. Garnish with cherry.

Californian- 1 1/2 oz vodka, 2-4 oz grapefruit juice, 2-4 oz orange juice, serve in a Collins glass with ice.

Caipirinha- 2 oz cachaca, 1 lime cut into 1/8ths, 2 tsps brown sugar. Put fruit in a Tumbler with sugar, muddle, fill glass with crushed ice, then add cachaca. Stir vigorously and serve with a straw.

Clover Club- 2 oz gin, 1 oz lemon juice, 1/2 oz raspberry syrup, shake 30 times in chilled ice shaker, pour into a Martini glass. Garnish with a lime.

Coladas- 1 1/2 oz coconut rum, 3-4 oz chosen fruit, 3-4 oz pineapple juice, 1 oz coconut syrup. Blend with ice and serve in a Tropical glass. Any fruit will do but the most popular Coladas use strawberry, pineapple or mango. Garnish with a cherry.

Cosmopolitan- 1 1/2 oz vodka, 3/4 oz Cointreau (or triple sec), 1/2 oz lime juice (lime cordial will work as well), 1/2 oz Ocean Spray Cranberry Juice, chill in shaker, pour into a Martini glass. Garnish with a lime.

Costa Del Sol- 1 1/2 oz sherry, 2 oz orange juice, 2 oz cream (or milk), 2 dashes of bitters. Shake with ice and serve in a Whiskey glass.

Cuba Libre- Build in a Collins glass with ice. 1 1/2 oz rum, fill with coke, always garnish with lime wedge or slice.

Daisy- Build in a Collins glass with ice. 2 1/2 oz gin, 1 oz lemon juice, 5-6 soda water, 1 dash of grenadine. Stir and serve. Garnish with a lime wedge.

Daiquiri- 1 1/2 oz rum, 3/4 lime juice, 3/4 oz simple syrup (later versions use triple sec), chill in shaker, pour in Cocktail glass, garnish with lime. Later versions were blended. Can be served on rocks.

RECIPES

Electric Blue- Build in a Tropical glass. 3/4 oz vodka, 3/4 oz gin, 3/4 oz white rum, 3/4 oz blue curacao, 1 oz lemon juice, 5-6 oz 7-Up. Shake and serve. Garnish with a lime.

Flamingo- 3/4 oz white rum, 3/4 oz spiced rum, 3/4 oz Licor 43, 2 oz Ocean Spray Ruby Red Grapefruit Juice. Shake and serve in a Whiskey glass.

Frisco- 2 oz rye whiskey, 1/4 oz Benedictine, 3/4 oz lemon juice. Put in shaker, chill, pour into a Martini glass. Garnish with a lemon twist.

French 75- 4 oz champagne, 1/4 oz gin, 1/4 oz Cointreau, 1/4 oz lemon juice. Shake gin, Cointreau, lemon juice in ice shaker, strain into Champagne glass, add champagne. Garnish with a lemon twist.

French Connection- 1 1/2 oz Grand Marnier, 1 1/2 cognac. Pour into a Brandy Snifter and serve.

Fuzzy Navel- Build in a Collins glass with ice. 1 1/2 oz peach schnapps, 5-6 oz orange juice. Garnish with an orange slice.

Gimlet- 2 1/2 oz gin, 1 oz lime cordial, chill in shaker, pour into a Martini glass. Garnish with a lime. This drink can also be served on ice.

SISKA
2 oz of Parma
6 oz of Ocean Spray Cranberry Juice
Splash of 7- Up
Garnish with Lime

Produced by Heaven Hill Distillers, PAMA is one of the best pomegranate liqueurs and is a favorite among the ladies. It hails from the Southern US.

RECIPES

Godfather- Build in a Whiskey glass with ice. 1 oz scotch, 3/4 oz amaretto.

Godmother- Build in a Whiskey glass with ice. 1 oz vodka, 3/4 oz amaretto.

Grasshopper- 1 oz of green creme de menthe, 1 oz white creme de cacao, 2-3 oz of Half/Half cream. Put in shaker, chill, pour into a Martini glass.

Green Eyed Monster- 2 oz Irish whiskey, 1/2 oz sweet vermouth, 1/4 oz Pernod, 1 dash of bitters. Put in shaker, chill, pour into a Martini glass. Garnish with a lemon twist.

Hot Toddy- 1 1/2 oz bourbon or rum, 1 tbsp honey, 2 oz lemon juice, 4-6 oz hot water. Heat ingredients and pour into a coffee mug.

Japanese Slipper- 3/4 oz sake, 3/4 oz Midori, 4-6 oz pineapple juice. Serve in a Collins glass.

Kamikazi- 1 oz vodka, 3/4 oz triple sec, 1/2 oz lime cordial, 1/2 oz lemon juice. Strain into a Martini glass. Garnish with a green lemon wedge.
* This drink can be turned into shooters.

Leap Year- 2 oz gin, 1/2 oz sweet vermouth, 1/2 oz Grand Marnier, 1/2 oz lemon juice. Put in shaker, chill, pour into a Martini glass. Garnish with a lemon twist.

Long Island Iced Tea- Build in a Tropical glass with ice. 3/4 oz vodka, 3/4 oz gin, 3/4 oz white rum, 3/4 oz tequila blanco, 3/4 oz triple sec, 1 1/2 oz lemon juice, 5-6 oz Coke. Stir and serve. Garnish with a lemon wedge.

Mai Tai- 1 oz white rum, 3/4 dark rum, 3/4 oz orange curacao, 1/2 oz orgeat syrup, 1/2 oz amaretto, 3-4 oz pineapple juice, 1-2 oz orange juice. Mix all ingredients except for dark rum together in a shaker. Pour into a Tropical glass and float dark rum on top. Garnish with a pineapple wedge and a cherry.

Manhattan- 2 oz whiskey (American or Canadian), 3/4 oz sweet vermouth, chill in shaker, pour into a Martini glass. Garnish with a cherry. Can be served on ice.

Margarita *frozen*- Salt the glass rim, 1 oz tequila, 1/2 oz triple sec, 3-4 oz sweetened lemon juice (or sweet sour mix - fresh is better) 3-5 oz ice. Put all in blender. If ice is too thick, add a little triple sec, it will make the ice thinner fast and also a little more lemon juice, then blend. If the drink is too thin, add ice slowly.

Adding fruit such as mango or strawberries is a great idea, but if frozen, treat them as ice and back-off the regular ice. Not frozen, treat fruit as juice and back-off from lemon juice. Do not put salt on fruit margaritas, rather sugar. Serve in a Margarita glass. Garnish with a lime.

RECIPES

Margarita *on the rocks*- Salt the glass rim, 1 oz tequila, 1/2 oz triple sec, 3-5 oz lemon juice, ice, mix in shaker, pour in a Whiskey glass. Garnish with a lime.

Martinez- 1 oz gin, 3/4 oz dry vermouth, 1/4 oz Cointreau, 2 dashes of bitters. Put in shaker, chill, pour into a Martini glass. Garnish with a lemon twist.

Melon Ball- Build in a Collins glass with ice. 3/4 oz vodka, 3/4 oz Midori Mellon Liqueur, 5-6 oz pineapple juice. Stir and serve. Garnish with a lime wedge.

Midori Sour- 1 1/2 oz Midori Melon Liqueur, 4-6 oz sweetened lemon juice, serve in Collins glass with ice. Garnish with lime.

Mint Julep- 3 oz bourbon, about 6 sprigs of mint leaves, 2 to 4 tablespoons of sugar, 2 to 4 oz soda or mineral water, garnish with mint. This drink needs the mint muddled first, add sugar, bourbon next, then add ice and top with soda water. Serve in a Mint Julep glass. Garnish with a sprig of mint.

MALIBU COFFEE
2 oz Malibu Caribbean Rum
1 oz Cream or Milk
5 - 6 oz Hot Coffee
Top with Whip Cream

When it's cold outside refreshingly cool drinks aren't what warms the insides, but a Malibu Coffee will do the trick. This Coconut Rum from Pernod Ricard is sweet enough to give the coffee an exotic flavor that can be enhanced with cream.

RECIPES

Mojito- 2 to 3 oz light rum, 1 lime, 1/2 oz simple syrup, 8 to 10 sprigs of mint. In a Whiskey glass put sugar and mint. Muddle. Cut lime in half, squeeze juice from both halves, leave one half in glass, add rum, then ice and fill with soda water. Garnish with a sprig of mint.

Monkey Gland- 1 1/2 oz gin, 1 1/2 oz orange juice, 1/4 oz anis liquor, 1/4 oz grenadine, chill in shaker, pour into a Martini glass. Garnish with an orange twist.

Moscow Mule- 2 oz vodka, 1 oz lime juice, 4 to 5 oz ginger beer or ginger ale. Pour ingredients into a Collins glass, add ice. Garnish with a lime wedge.

Negroni- 1 oz gin, 1 oz sweet vermouth, 1 oz Compari. Put in shaker, chill, pour into a Martini glass. Garnish with an orange twist.

New Orleans Buck- Build in a Collins glass with ice. 1 1/2 oz white rum, 1 oz lime juice, 1 oz orange juice, 3 dashes bitters, 3-4 oz ginger ale. Garnish with a lime wedge.

"Absinthe makes the tart grow fonder."

- Ernest Dowson

Old Fashioned- Build in a Whiskey glass. 2 oz whiskey (American or Canadian), 2 dashes Angostura bitters, 1 teaspoon of sugar, cherry, orange wheel. Fruit and sugar should be muddled (mashed together) in bottom of glass, bitters added, then ice, only then add spirits. Stir lightly.

Orgasm- Build in a Collins glass with ice. 3/4 oz dark creme de cacao, 3/4 oz amaretto, 3/4 oz triple sec, 3/4 oz vodka, 4-6 oz Half/Half cream. Shake and serve. Top with whipped cream.

Perfect Manhattan- 2 oz bourbon, 1/4 oz sweet vermouth, 1/4 oz dry vermouth, 1 dash of bitters. Put in shaker, chill, pour into a Martini glass. Garnish with a lemon twist.

Rickey- Build in a Collins glass with ice. 1 1/2 oz rum, vodka, OR gin, 1 oz lemon juice, 5-6 oz club soda. Garnish with a lemon wedge.

Rising Sun- Build in a Collins glass. 1 1/2 oz sake, 1 oz orange juice, 3-4 oz Ocean Spray Cranberry Juice. Pour orange juice first, then sake, then add Ocean Spray Cranberry Juice.

Rob Roy- Build in a Whiskey glass. 2 oz scotch, 1/4 - 1/2 oz sweet vermouth. Serve on ice. Garnish with a cherry.

Rusty Nail- Build in a Whiskey glass. 1 1/2 oz scotch, 1/2 to 1 oz (according to taste) Drambuie.

Sake Gimlet- Build in a Whiskey glass with ice. 2 oz sake, 1-2 oz lime cordial.

RECIPES

Sakitini- 3/4 oz vodka, 3/4 oz sake with olives or lemon twist. Serve chilled in a Martini glass.

Satan's Whiskers- 3/4 oz gin, 3/4 oz dry vermouth, 3/4 oz sweet vermouth, 1/2 oz Grand Marnier, 1/2 oz orange juice, 1 dash of orange bitters. Put in shaker, chill, pour into a Martini glass. Garnish with an orange twist.

Savoy- 1 1/2 oz gin, 1/2 oz dry vermouth, 2 dashes of Dubonnet. Put in shaker, chill, pour into a Martini glass. Garnish with an orange twist.

Sho Gun- Build in a Whiskey glass with ice. 1 1/2 oz vodka, 1/2 oz Midori Melon Liqueur.

Side Car- 1 1/2 oz cognac, 3/4 oz Cointreau, 3/4 oz lemon juice, chill in shaker, rim cocktail glass with sugar, pour into a Martini glass. Garnish with a lemon wedge.

Silk Panties- Build in a Collins glass with ice. 1 oz peach schnapps, 1 oz vodka, 4-5 oz Ocean Spray Cranberry Juice. Garnish with a lime wedge.

Slippery Nipple- Build in a 1 1/2 oz Shot glass. 3/4 oz sambuca, 3/4 oz Bailey's Irish Cream.

Spanish Fizz- 1 1/2 oz sherry, 2 oz sweetened lemon juice, 4-6 oz soda water served in Collins glass with ice.

Springbok- Build in a 1 1/2 oz Shot glass. 3/4 oz green creme de menthe, 3/4 oz Bailey's Irish Cream.

Tequila Sunrise- Build in a Collins glass with ice. 1 1/2 oz tequila, 4-5 oz orange juice, 1/2 oz grenadine. Add tequila, grenadine and orange juice in order. Garnish with a cherry.

Toasted Almond- Build in a Collins glass with ice. 1 oz Kalua, 1 oz amaretto, 4-5 oz milk. Shake and serve.

CREAMY SYMPHONY
1 1/2 to 2 oz of any Mozart product
Gold, Black, White
1/2 oz of Mozart Choco/Orange
6 - 7 oz of Milk or Half and Half
The Creamy Symphony is almost like drinking a dessert.

RECIPES

Tom Collins- Build in a Collins glass with ice. 2 oz gin, 1 oz lemon juice, 1 tsp simple syrup, 5-6 oz soda water. Stir and serve. Garnish with a lemon twist.

Usa Rose- Build in a Whiskey glass. 1 oz Midori Mellon Liqueur, 4-6 oz Ocean Spray Cranberry Juice. Garnish with a lime.

Valencia Rose- 1 oz Licor 43, 4-6 oz Ocean Spray Cranberry Juice. Serve with ice in Collins glass.

Waikiki- 1 1/2 rum, 3/4 oz blue curacao, 1 oz coconut cream, 3-4 oz pineapple juice. Put in shaker, chill, pour into a Martini glass. Garnish with a lemon twist.

Ward 8- 2 oz bourbon, 1/2 oz lemon juice, 1/2 oz orange juice, 1 tsp grenadine. Put in shaker, chill, pour into a Martini glass. Garnish with a lemon twist.

White Russian- Build in a Collins glass with ice. 3/4 oz Kahlua, 3/4 oz vodka, 5-6 oz Half/Half cream. Shake and serve.

Woo Woo- Build in a Collins ice with ice. 3/4 oz vodka, 3/4 oz peach schnapps, 5-6 oz Ocean Spray Cranberry Juice. Stir and serve. Garnish with a lime wedge.

COFFEE AND TEA

Irish Coffee #1- 1 cup of coffee, 1 oz Irish whiskey. Cherry can be added at discretion. Serve in a Coffee glass. Top with whipped cream.

Irish Coffee #2- 1 cup of coffee, 1 oz Kahlua, 1 oz Irish whiskey. Cherry can be added at discretion. Serve in a Coffee glass. Top with whipped cream.

French Connection Coffee- 1 cup of coffee, 1 oz cognac, 1 oz Grand Marnier. Stir and serve in a Coffee glass. Top with whipped cream.

Captain's Coffee- 1 cup of coffee, 1 oz Bailey's Irish Cream, 1 oz Captain Morgan's Spiced Rum. Stir and serve in a Coffee glass. Top with whipped cream.

Coffee Side Car- 1 cup of coffee, 1 oz cognac, 1 oz Cointreau, 1 oz milk. Stir and serve in a Coffee glass. Top with whipped cream.

Bourbon and Crème- 1 cup of coffee, 1 oz bourbon, 1 oz Crème de Cacao Liqueur. Stir and serve in a Coffee glass. Top with whipped cream.

Mudslide Coffee- 1 cup of coffee, 1 oz Bailey's Irish Cream, 1 oz Kahlua. Stir and serve in a Coffee glass. Top with whipped cream.

Coco Loco Coffee- 1 cup of coffee, 1 oz coconut rum, 1 oz Bailey's Irish Cream. Stir and serve in a Coffee glass. Top with whipped cream.

RECIPES

Orange Jasmine- 1 cup of orange jasmine tea, 1 oz B&B, 1 teaspoon of clover honey. Stir and serve in a Coffee glass.

Nippon Milk Tea- 1 cup of orange jasmine tea, 1 1/2 oz Midori Mellon Liqueur, 1/2 oz Bailey's Irish Cream. Stir and serve in a Coffee glass.

MARTINIS

5th Avenue- 3/4 oz vodka, 3/4 oz apricot brandy, 3/4 oz white crème de cacao. Put in shaker, chill, pour into a Martini glass.

Aviation- 1 1/2 oz gin, 1/2 oz maraschino liqueur, 3/4 oz lemon juice, chill, then pour into a Martini glass. Garnish with a cherry and a lemon twist. This is a classic from the Rainbow Room in New York. Called the "prince of classic cocktails". Hard to find now because many bars don't have maraschino.

Cantaloupe Martini- 1 1/2 oz vodka, 1/2 oz watermelon liqueur, 1 oz lemon juice, 2 oz orange juice. Put in shaker, chill, pour into a Martini glass. Garnish with an orange twist.

Chocolate Martini- 1 1/4 oz vodka, 3/4 oz white crème de cacao. Put in shaker, chill, pour into a Martini glass.

Classic Martini- 2 1/2 oz gin, 1/2 oz dry vermouth. Put in shaker, chill, pour into a Martini glass. Garnish with olives. To make a "Dirty Martini", add a little of the brine from the olive jar. Very Dirty means more brine. This makes the drink salty.

Espresso Martini- 1 oz vanilla schnapps, 3/4 oz vodka, 3/4 oz Kahlua, 3 oz chilled espresso coffee. Put in shaker, chill, pour into a Martini glass. Garnish with 3 coffee beans.

Full Moon Martini- 1 oz Grand Marnier, 1 1/2 oz amaretto, 3 oz orange juice. Put in shaker, chill, pour into a Martini glass.

Gibson- 2 oz gin, 1/4 oz dry vermouth. Put in shaker, chill, pour into a Martini glass. Garnish with a white cocktail onion. The onion makes this a Gibson instead of a Martini.

Oatmeal Cookie- 1 oz Jagermeister, 1 oz cinnamon liqueur, 1 oz butterscotch liqueur, 1 1/2 oz Bailey's Irish Cream. Put in shaker, chill, pour into a Martini glass.

Peaches and Cream- 1 oz peach schnapps, 1 oz vodka, 3-4 oz of Half/Half cream. Put in shaker, chill, pour into a Martini glass. Garnish with whipped cream.

Perfect Martini- 2 oz gin, 1/2 oz dry vermouth, 1/2 oz sweet vermouth. Put in shaker, chill, pour into a Martini glass. Garnish with olives or a lemon twist.

RECIPES

Recipes from page 7:

Pink Gin- 3 oz gin, 2 dashes of bitters. Put gin in shaker and chill. Put bitters in a Martini glass and swirl, then add gin. This was the drink of choice for Ian Fleming during his press interviews.

Spanish Vodka Martini- 2 1/2 oz vodka, 1 tbsp of sherry. Put in shaker, chill, pour into a Martini glass. Garnish with a lemon twist.

Vesper- 2 oz gin, 1 oz vodka, 1/2 oz Lillet. chill in shaker. Put in shaker, chill, pour into a Martini glass. This drink came from James Bond in "Casino Royal".

Far Eastern Gimlet- 1 1/2 oz of dry gin, 1/8 oz of simple syrup, 1/16 oz of Rose's Lime Cordial, 3 oz of water. Build all into a Rocks glass with ice. Stir gently until mixed. Garnish with a lime wheel.

Tiger's Milk- 3 oz of VSOP or XO Cognac, 1/2 oz simple syrup, 3 oz cream, 3 oz milk. Shake briskly with ice before straining into glass. Can garnish with nutmeg if desired.

Rosy Dawn Cocktail- 1 oz dry gin, 1 oz orange curacao, 1 oz cherry brandy, 1/8 oz Rose's Lime Cordial, 1 oz soda water. Put ingredients (except soda water) in 6 oz Tumbler with cracked ice. Stir ingredients and then add soda water. Stir again.

Russian Cocktail- 2 oz VSOP Cognac, 2 oz Kummel, 6 oz champagne. Put Cognac and Kummel into a 10 oz Goblet filled with fine cracked ice. Stir. Add champagne. Garnish with flower bloom of your choice.

Shanghai Buck- Build in a Collins glass with ice. 1 1/2 oz white rum, 2 dashes bitters, 1/2 tbsp grenadine, 1 oz lime juice, 5-6 oz ginger ale. Stir and garnish with a lime.

HENDRICK'S MARTINI
3 - 4 oz of Hendrick's Gin
With its smooth hint of cucumber the best way to enjoy this gem is to chill it and serve it alone.

"The difference between Cocktails and Aperitifs is chiefly that Cocktails are always mixtures of a number of different ingredients, so well blended together that not any one of them overshadows the other."

- Andre Simon, Early 20th Century French Wine Merchant

TASTE GLOSSARY

A World of Taste

There's a whole world of taste out there waiting for someone to mix it up. While you might not be able to find everything in the following section at the local store at least you'll have an idea of the qualities that make it popular in its native land.

Distilled spirits are integrated with all forms of human culture and knowing what people drink in their homeland is the next best thing to having it on the shelf behind you.

Drinking Alone under the Moon

A jug of wine amidst the flowers;
Drinking alone, with no friend near.
Raising my cup, I beckon the bright moon;
My shadow included, we're a party of three.
Although the moon's unused to drinking
And the shadow only apes my every move
For the moment I'll just take them as they are,
Enjoying spring when spring is here.
Reeling shadow, swaying moon
Attend my dance and song.
Still sober, we rejoice together;
Drunk, each takes his leave.
To seal forever such unfettered friendship
Let's rendezvous beyond the Milky Way.

- Li Bai, 8th Century Chinese Poet

TASTE GLOSSARY

NAME	SOURCE	TYPE	COLOR	TASTE
Absinth	Bohemia, Various	Liqueur	Green	Licorice
Advocaat	Holland	Prepared Eggnog	Yellow	Sweet
Aiguebelle	France	Liqueur	Green/Yellow	Herbal
Alize	France	Liqueur	Yellow, Blue, Red	Sweet, Passion fruit
Alpenkraeuterlikoer	Germany	Liqueur	Brownish/ Yellow	Herbal
Amaretto	Italy, Various	Liqueur	Brown Almond	Sweet
Amer Picon	France	Aperitif	Amber	Bitter
Angostura Bitters	Trinidad	Bitters	Redish Brown	Bitter
Anisette	Various	Liqueur	White	Sweet
Applejack	U.S.	Apple Brandy	Amber	Dry, Fruity
Apricot Liqueur	Various	Liqueur	Amber	Sweet, Fruity
Aquavit	Denmark	Spirit	White	Caraway
Armagnac	Germany, France	Brandy	Amber	Dry
Baerenfang	Germany	Liiqueur	Golden Yellow	Sweet, Honey
Bailey's	Ireland	Liqueur	Cream	Sweet
Bal Jui	China	Spirit	Clear	Dry, Bitter
Barack Palinka	Hungary	Brandy	Orange	Dry, Apricot
Batavia Arak	Indonesia	Spirit	Straw	Dry
Benedictine	France	Liqueur	Gold	Sweet, Spicy
Bergamottelikoer	Germany	Liqueur	Yellowish-Green	Citrus, Herbal

TASTE GLOSSARY

NAME	SOURCE	TYPE	COLOR	TASTE
B & B	France	Liqueur	Gold	Sweet, Spicy
Bitters	Various	Spirit	Reddish Brown	Bitter
Blackberry Liqueur	Various	Liqueur	Dark Red	Sweet
Boukha	North Africa	Aperitif	Clear	Fig, Spicy
Bourbon Whiskey	U.S.	Spirit	Brown	Dry
Brandy	Various	Fruit Spirit	Amber	Dry, Fruity
Byrrh	France	Aperitif	Clear	Sweet, Bitter
Calvados	France	Apple Brandy	Brown	Dry, Fruity
Campari	Italy	Aperitif	Red	Bitter
Canadian Whiskey	Canada	Spirit	Brown	Dry, Rich
Cap Corse	Corsica	Aperitif	Reddish-Brown	Fruity, Vanilla
Celtic Crossing	Ireland	Liqueur	Amber	Sweet, Brandy
Cerasella	Italy	Liqueur	Red	Cherry, Herbal
Chajiu	China	Spirit	Reddish Brown	Tea, Dry
Chambord	France	Liqueur	Dark Red	Raspberry
Chartreuse	France	Liqueur	Yellow, Green	Spicy, Sweet
Cherry Liqueur	Various	Liqueur	Red	Sweet, Cherry
CocoRibe	Virgin Islands	Liqueur	White	Sweet, Coconut
Cointreau	France	Liqueur	White	Sweet
Creme d'Ananas	Various	Liqueur	Pale Yellow	Pineapple

TASTE GLOSSARY

NAME	SOURCE	TYPE	COLOR	TASTE
Crème de Bananes	Various	Liqueur	Gold	Sweet
Crème de Cacao	Various	Liqueur	Brown, White	Sweet
Crème de Cassis	Various	Liqueur	Red	Sweet
Crème de Menthe	Various	Liqueur	White or Green	Sweet, Mint
Creme de Noisette	Various	Liqueur	Amber	Nutty, Sweet
Creme mit Nuss	German	Liqueur	Brown	Chocolate
Crème de Noyaux	Various	Liqueur	Pink	Sweet, Nut
Crème de Violettes	Various	Liqueur	Violet	Sweet
Crème de Yvette	Various	Liqueur	Violet	Sweet
Cuarenta Y Tres	Spain	Liqueur	Straw	Sweet, Vanilla
Cumin	Various	Liqueur	Clear	Spicy, Cummin
Curacao	Various	Liqueur	Orange	Sweet, Orange
Cynar	Italy	Aperitif	Brown	Bitter
Danzige Goldwasser	Germany	Liqueur	White	Sweet
Demeraran Rum	Guyana	Spirit	Dark Brown	Dry
Drambuie	Scotland	Liqueur	Gold	Sweet, Spicy
Dubonnet	France	Aperitif	Red	Sweet
Eau de Vie De Marc	France	Brandy	Brown	Dry
Eau de Vie	Various	Pear	White	Dry, Pear
Ergoutou	China	Spirit	Clear	Dry, Bitter

TASTE GLOSSARY

NAME	SOURCE	TYPE	COLOR	TASTE
Feng Xiang	China	Spirit	Gold	Honey, Sweet
Fernet	Italy	Bitters	Reddish	Bitter
Fior d'Alpe	Italy	Liqueur	Gold	Sweet
Fraise	Various	Strawberry Brandy	White	Dry, Strawberry
Framboise	Various	Raspberry Brandy	White	Dry, Raspberry
Frangelico	Italy	Liqueur	Straw	Sweet, Hazelnut
French Vermouth	France	Aperitif	White	Dry
Galliano	Italy	Liqueur	Yellow	Sweet
Genever (Gin)	Holland	Spirit	White	Dry
Gin, dry	Various	Spirit	White	Dry
Godiva	France	Liqueur	Creamy Brown	Chocolate
Goldschlager	Switzerland	Liqueur	White, Gold Flake	Cinnamon
Gouqi jiu	China	Spirit	Red	Dry Wolfberry
Grand Marnier	France	Liqueur	Orange	Sweet, Orange
Haitian Rum	Haiti	Spirit	Straw	Dry
Hollands (gin)	Holland	Spirit	White	Dry
Houx	Various	Liqueur	Clear	Dry, Holly Berry
Irish Mist	Ireland	Liqueur	Straw	Sweet
Irish Whiskey	Ireland	Spirit	Brown	Dry
Italian Vermouth	Italy	Aperitif	Redish Brown	Bittersweet

TASTE GLOSSARY

NAME	SOURCE	TYPE	COLOR	TASTE
Jaegermiester	Germany	Aperitif	Brown	Bitter, Sweet
Jamaican Rum	Jamaica	Spirit	Dark Brown	Dry
Karpi	Finland	Liqueur	Clear	Cranberry, Dry
Kahlua	Mexico	Liqueur	Brown	Sweet, Coffee
Kirsch	Various	Brandy	Cherry White	Dry, Cherry
Kirschwasser	Various	Brandy	Cherry White	Dry, Cherry
Koumiss	Various	Fermented Milk	White	Dry, Spicy
Kummel	Various	Liqueur	White	Sweet, Caraway
Liqueur d'or	Various	Liqueur	Clear/Gold Flakes	Spicy
Lillet	France	Aperitif	White	Bitter
Malibu Rum	Caribbean	Spirit	White	Sweet, Coconut
Maraschino	Various	Liqueur	White	Sweet, Cherry
Mastikha	Greece	Liqueur	Cloudy, White	Sweet
Meiguilu jiu	China	Spirit	Clear, Rose,	Dry
Midori	Japan	Liqueur	Green	Sweet, Melon
Mirabelle	Various	Liqueur	Clear	Dry, Plum
Maotai	China	Spirit	Clear	Dry
Mozart	Austria	Liqueur	Brown	Chocolate
Myrtille	Various	Liqueur	Clear, Dry	Blueberry
Okolehao	Hawaii	Spirit	Amber	Dry, Spicy

TASTE GLOSSARY

NAME	SOURCE	TYPE	COLOR	TASTE
Opal Nera Sambuca	Italy	Liqueur	Dark Purple	Sweet, Licorice
Ouzo	Greece	Liqueur	Cloudy White	Sweet, Licorice
Passoa	Brazil	Liqueur	Red	Passion Fruit
Pastis de Marseilles	France	Liqueur	Cloudy White	Sweet, Licorice
Peach Liqueur	Various	Liqueur	Brown	Sweet, Fruity
Pernod	France	Liqueur	Gree Gold	Sweet, Licorice
Peter Heering	Denmark	Liqueur	Red	Sweet, Cherry
Phai Thong	Thailand	Spirit	Clear	Dry
Pi Lu Chiew	China	Liqueur	Green	Sweet, Herbal
Pousse-Café	France	Liqueur	Various	Sweet
Prunelle	France	Liqueur	Brown	Sweet, Plum
Puerto Rican Rum	Puerto Rico	Spirit	White	Dry
Quinquina	France	Aperitif	Red or White	Bittersweet
Raki	Turkey	Liqueur	White	Sweet, Licorice
Ricard	France	Liqueur	Brown	Semisweet
Rock and Rye	U.S.	Liqueur	Amber	Sweet Whiskey
Ruang Kao	Spirit	Thailand	Clear	Dry
Rum	Various	Spirit	Various	Dry, Sweet
Rumple Minze	Germany	Liqueur	White	Sweet, Mint

TASTE GLOSSARY

NAME	SOURCE	TYPE	COLOR	TASTE
Sake	Japan	Rice Wine	Clear	Dry, Bitter
Sabra	Israel	Liqueur	Brown	Sweet Chocolate
Saint-Raphael	France	Aperitif	Red	Bitter
Sambuca	Italy	Liqueur	Cloudy White	Sweet, Licorice
Sanhua jiu	China	Spirit	Greenish Yellow	Dry, Herbal
Scheidam (Gin)	Holland	Spirit	White	Dry
Scotch Whisky	Scotland	Spirit	Brown	Dry, Smoky
Seve	France	Liqueur	Orange	Herb, Spicy
Sheridan	Ireland	Liqueur	Black or White	Chocolate
Sho-chu	Japan	Spirit	Clear	Dry
Slivovitz	Various	Plum Brandy	Brown	Dry, Plum
Sloe Gin	England	Liqueur	Red	Sweet
Soju	Korea	Spirit	Clear	Dry, Bitter
Southern Comfort	U.S.	Liqueur	Amber	Sweet, Whiskey
Strega	Italy	Liqueur	Gold	Sweet
Suze	France	Aperitif	Brown	Bittersweet
Swedish Punsch	Sweden	Liqueur	Yellow	Sweet
Tequila	Mexico	Spirit	White	Dry Gold
Tia Maria	Jamaica	Liqueur	Brown	Sweet, Coffee

TASTE GLOSSARY

NAME	SOURCE	TYPE	COLOR	TASTE
To Mei Chiew	China	Clear	Sweet	Flower
Toddy	India	Spirit	Clear	Dry
Tuba	Philippines	Spirit	Clear	Dry
Triple Sec	Various	Liqueur	White	Sweet, Orange
Tuaca	Italy	Liqueur	Brown	Sweet
Van Der Hum	South Africa	Liqueur	Gold	Sweet
Vandermint	Holland	Liqueur	Creamy Brown	Chocolate Mint
Vodka	Various	Spirit	White	Dry
Whisky	Various	Spirit	Brown	Dry
Wisniowka	Poland	Liqueur	Red	Sweet, Cherry
Yukon Jack	Canada	Liqueur	Brown	Sweet, Whiskey
Zhuyeqing jiu	China	Spirit	Clear	Sweet, Dry
Zubrowka	Russia	Flavored Spirit	Straw	Dry

"I have heard people complain their wine was 'corked' when they found a fragment of broken cork floating in the glass. When wine is truly 'corky' the cork is diseased and foul-smelling and the wine is more or less tainted. It should never be drunk in this condition...it is for this reason that a small quantity of wine is invariably poured first into the host's glass for him to taste...If the host is so barbarous as to taste and accept a corky wine, all that the guest can do is to refrain from drinking it and never come to that table again."

- Evelyn Waugh, Wine In Peace and Ward, 1949

RECOMMENDED READING

100 Famous Cocktails
et. al. Oscar of the Waldorf
Kenilworth Press, Inc, 1934

Alcoholica Esoterica
Lendler, Ian
Penguin Books, 2005
ISBN 0-14-303597-5

Atomic Cocktails: Mixed Drinks for Modern Times
Brooks, Karen, and Bosker, Gideon, and Darmon, Reed
Chronicle Books, 1998
ISBN 0-8118-1926-4

Bacchus Behave! The Lost Art of Polite Drinking
Whitaker, Alma
Frederick A. Stokes Company, 1933

Barkeeper's Golden Book
ed. Blunier, O
Morgarten-Verlag A.G., 1935

Bartender's Guide
Vic, Trader
Garden City Books, 1947

Classic Cocktail of the Prohibition Era
Collins, Philip
W. Quay Hays, 1997
ISBN 1-57544-020-2

Cocktail and Wine Digest
Haimo, Oscar
The Cocktail, Wine, Beer and Spirit Digest, 1945

Cocktail, The Drinks Bible for the 21st Century
Harrihgton, Paul and Moorhead, Laura
Viking Press, 1998
ISBN 0-670-88022-1

Dictionary of Wines and Spirits
Price, Pamela Vandyke
Peerage Books, 1986
ISBN 1-85052-053-4

Grossman's Guide to Wines, Spirits and Beers
Grossman, Harold
Charlses Scribners's Sons, 1964
Library of Congress Catalogue # 64-24895

Here's How: Mixed Drinks
Compiled by Whitfield, W.C.
Three Mountaineers, Inc. 1941

RECOMMENDED READING

Jim Murray's Whiskey Bible
Murrray, Jim
Carlton Books, 2006

Michael Jackson's Malt Whiskey Companion
Jackson, Michael
Dorling Kindersley, 1999
ISBN 0-7513-0708-4

Mr. Boston's Bartender and Party Guide
Warner Books, 1997
ISBN 0-446-67042-1

New Classic Cocktails
Regan, Gary and Regan, Mardee Haidin
Macmillan, 1997
ISBN 0-02-861349-X

Official Mixer's Manual
Duffy, Patrick
Blue Ribbon Books, 1940

Old Waldorf Bar Days
Crockett, Albert
Aventine Press, 1931

Playboy's Host & Bar Book
Mario, Thomas
Playboy Press, 1971

Seagram's Bartending Guide
Viking, 1995
ISBN 0-670-86397-1

Shaken and Stirred
Hamilton, William L. Hamilton
Harper Collins, 2004
ISBN 0-06-074044-2

Ted Saucier's Bottom's Up, New and Revised Edition
Hawthorn Books, 1962

The American Drink Book
Field, SS
Kingsport Press, 1953

The Art of Drinking, What and How
Mason, Dexter
Farrar and Rihehart, 1930

The Bartender's Bible
Regan, Gary
Harper Collins, 1991
ISBN 0-06-016722-X

The Bartender's Companion: A Complete Recipe Guide
e.d. Plotkin, Robert
P.S.D. Publishing Inc., DBA, 1997
ISBN 0-945562-22-5

RECOMMENDED READING

The Bon Vivant's Campanion, How to Mix Drinks
Thomas, Jerry (Professor)
Alfred A. Knopf, 1928

The Bon Vivant's Companion
Zabriskie, George
The Doldrums, 1948

The Craft of the Cocktail
DeGroff, Dale
Clarkson Potter Publishers, 2002
ISBN 0-609-60875-4

The Fine Art of Mixing Drinks
Embry, David
Doubleday and company, 1958

The Flowing Bowl
Spencer, Edward
Stanley Paul & Co, Ltd. Reprinted, 1925

**The Gentlemen's Companion:
An Exotic Drinking Book**
Baker, Charles, Jr.
Derrydale Press, Inc, 1992 Limited Edition

The Joy of Drinking
Holland, Barbara
Bloomsbury USA, 2007
ISBN 1-59691-337-1

The Old Waldorf-Astoria Bar Book
Crockett, A.S.
New Day Publishing, Reprinted, 1935

The Pocket Bartender's Guide
Jackson, Michael
Simon and Schuster, 1979
ISBN 0-671-2508-7

Wild West Bartender's Bible
Johnson, Byron and Sharon
Texas Monthly Press, 1986
ISBN 0-87719-050-0

*Alcohol's a temptress,
Alcohol's a flirt,
She'll either raise you to the skies,
Or drop you to the dirt.*

*- ABC of Cocktails
Peter Pauper Press, 1953*

2008 SALES RANKINGS

The Top 5 Global Spirits ranked by Cases Sold

1 Jinro, a soju owned by Hite, produced in South Korea.

Sixty-million cases in 2007.

2 Ruang Khao, a Thai spirit owned by Thai Beverage, produced in Thailand.

Thirty-five million cases in 2007.

3 Ginebra, a gin owned by San Miguel, produced in the Philippines.

Twenty-five million cases in 2007.

4 Smirnoff, a vodka owned by Diageo, produced in the United States.

Twenty-two million cases in 2007.

5 Cachaca 51, a cachaca owned by Industrias Muller de Beidas, produced in Brazil.

Twenty-million cases in 2007.

Source: IMPACT

Top 2 Global Products by Type

Vodka:
#1 Smirnoff, owned by Diageo
#2 Absolut, owned by Pernod Ricard

Rum:
#1 Bacardi, owned by Bacardi
#2 Tanduay, owned Tanduay Distilleries

Gin:
#1 Ginebra, owned by San Miguel
#2 Gordon's, owned by Diageo

Tequila:
#1 Jose Cuervo, owned by Grupa Tequila Cuervo
#2 Sauza, owned Beam Global

Whisky:
#1 Jonnie Walker, owned by Diageo
#2 Bagpiper, owned by United Spirits

Liqueur:
#1 Bailey's, owned by Diageo
#2 Jagermeister, owned by Mast Jagermeister ***

*** Technically Jagermeister is a bitters but it's often used as a liqueur in cocktails.

Source: IMPACT

COMPANY & BRAND INDEX

The global spirits industry is just as dynamic as it is mature. Like a good whiskey aging in a barrel, its flavor becoming more complex over time, this industry has grown and changed to the extent that today it can seem a little mysterious - even to people that work within its sphere.

There is more than one reason for this complexity but it can be summed-up nicely by the term evolution. Like anything that has been around for generations, the spirits industry bares some of the nomenclature and semiotics of the past, mixed with modern corporate culture and a whole lot of marketing.

It's important to be in-touch with marketing initiatives, but even more important to know your products and who owns them. Accurate product knowledge helps bars identify trends, gain valuable corporate marketing assistance, and be in the driver's seat when talking to distributors. The following is an index of companies from around the world and the brands they are currently holding. As this list will always be dynamic, watch it evolve on www.cocktailcool. com to stay as current as possible.

The Top 20 Global Spirits Companies ranked by Market Share

1   Diageo PLC ***
2   Pernod Ricard Groupe ***
3   Hite Brewery Co Ltd
4   UB Group
5   Thai Beverage PLC
6   Bacardi & Co Ltd
7   Fortune Brands Inc
8   Cia Müller de Bebidas
9   San Miguel Corp
10 Doosan Group
11 Sichuan Yibin Wuliangye Distillery Co Ltd
12 Brown-Forman Corp
13 Takara Holdings Inc
14 V&S Vin & Sprit AB ***
15 Engarrafamento Pitú Ltda
16 Tanduay Distillers Inc
17 CL World Brands Ltd
18 Suntory Ltd
19 Constellation Brands Inc
20 Campari Milano SpA, Davide
21 Asahi Breweries Ltd ***

*** Pernod Ricard purchased Vin and Sprit in early 2008. When the sale is sorted, there is a strong chance Pernod Ricard will take over Diageo as number 1. That would make Asahi number 20.

Compiled by Euromonitor 2008

1921 Tequila

1921 White

1921 Aged

1921 Rerseva Especial

Tequila Cream

AB Stumbras

Brandy Gloria 5 Year Old

Brandy Gloria 7 Year Old

Brandy Gloria 10 Year Old

Herbal Bitter 999

Herbal Liqueur Green 999

Honey liqueur Krupnikas

Liqueur Lithuanian Amber Vodka & Caramel

Liqueur Lithuanian Black Vodka & Black Currant

Liqueur Lithuanian Red Vodka & Cranberry

Liqueur Poema Royal Plum

Liqueur Žagares' Cherry

Original Lithuanian Vodka

Original Lithuanian Cherry Vodka

Original Lithuanian Cranberry Vodka

Original Lithuanian Gold Vodka

Original Lithuanian Raspberry Vodka

Ozone Vodka

Pear-flavored Brandy Gloria

Plum-flavored Brandy Gloria

Stumbras Buffalo grass Vodka

Stumbras Centenary Vodka

Stumbras Rye-Bread Vodka

Special liqueur Stumbro Starka

Asahi Breweries

Nikka Brandy VSOP

Nikka Brandy XO

Nikka Whisky

Bali Moon Liqueurs

Bali Moon Banana Liqueur

Bali Moon Blue Curacao

Bali Moon Coffee Liqueur

Bali Moon Coconut Liqueur

Bali Moon Melon Liqueur

Bali Moon Pineapple Liqueur

Bali Moon Triple Sec

Bali Moon Vodka

Bacardi

42 Below

Aberfeldy

Amarula

Aultmore

B & B

Bacardi 151

Bacardi 1873

Bacardi 8

Bacardi Añejo

Bacardi Big Apple

*"Here's to you and to me
And thirsty souls where'er they may be."*

- Toast - Anonymous

Bacardi

Bacardi Cocó

Bacardi Grand Melon

Bacardi Limón

Bacardi Peach Red

Bacardi O

Bacardi Oro (Gold)

Bacardi Reserva

Bacardi Reserva Limitada

Bacardi Razz

Bacardi Select (previously "Bacardi Black")

Bacardi Silver

Bacardi Superior

Benedictine

Bombay Dry

Bombay Sapphire

Cazadores Tequila

Craigellachie

Dewars White Label

Dewar's 12

Dewar's 18 Founder's Reserve

Dewar's Signature

Disaronno Amaretto

Drambuie

Eristoff vodka

Eristoff Red

Eristoff Black

Eristoff Limskaya

Glen Deveron

Grey Goose Vodka

Grey Goose L'Orange

Grey Goose Le Citron

Grey Goose La Poire

Martini and Rossi

Noilly Prat

Otard Cognac

Royal Brackla

South Gin

Constellation Spirits

1792 Ridgemont Reserve Small Batch Bourbon

99 Apples Schnapps

99 Bananas Schnapps

99 Blackberries Schnapps

99 Black Cherries

99 Oranges Schnapps

Balblair Single Malt Scotch

Barton California Brandy

Barton California Deluxe

Barton Gin

Barton Gold Rum

Barton Light Rum

Barton Long Island Iced Tea

Barton Peach Schnapps

Barton Premium Blend

Barton Reserve Blend

Constellation Spirits

Barton Tequila

Barton Triple Sec

Barton Vodka

Barton's Canadian

Barton's Tequila and Triple Sec

Black Velvet Canadian

Black Velvet Reserve

Blue Wave Vodka

Calypso Gold Rum

Calypso Light Rum

Canadian Host

Canadian LTD

Canadian Supreme

Capitan Gold Tequila

Capitan Tequila & Triple Sec

Capitan White Tequila

Caravella Limoncello

Caravella Orangecello

Cherry Wave Vodka

Chi-Chi's Appletini

Chi-Chi's Caribbean Mudslide

Chi-Chi's Cosmopolitan

Chi-Chi's Lemon Drop

Chi-Chi's Long Island Iced Tea

Chi-Chi's Mai Tai

Chi-Chi's Mango Margarita

Chi-Chi's Mexican Mudslide

Chi-Chi's Original Margarita

Chi-Chi's Piña Colada

Chi-Chi's Premium Gold Margarita

Chi- Chi's Strawberry Daiquiri

Chi-Chi's Strawberry Margarita

Chi-Chi's Vanilla Mudslide

Chi-Chi's White Russian

Corby's Canadian

Corby's Reserve Blend

Crystal Palace Gin

Crystal Palace Vodka

Czarina Gin

Czarina Vodka

Danfield's Canadian Whisky

Amaretto di Amore

Raspberry di Amore

Sambuca di Amore

Effen Vodka

Effen Black Cherry Vodka

Effen Raspberry Vodka

El Toro Tequila

El Toro Tequila Reposado

El Toro Tequila Triple Distilled Silver

Fleischmann's Brandy

Fleischmann's Flavored Vodkas

Fleischmann's Gin

Fleischmann's Preferred Blend

Fleischmann's Rum

Constellation Spirits

Fleischmann's Rye

Fleischmann's Vodka

Glenmore Gin

Glenmore Vodka

Hartley Brandy

Highland Mist Scotch

House of Stuart Scotch

Imperial Blend

Inver House Scotch

Jacques Bonet Brandy

Kentucky Gentleman Bourbon-A-Blend

Kentucky Tavern Bourbon

Lauder's Scotch

MacNaughton Canadian

McMaster's Canadian

McMaster's Scotch

Meukow VO Cognac

Meukow VSOP Cognac

Meukow Vanilla Cognac Liqueur

Meukow 90

Meukow XO

Monte Alban Mezcal

Montezuma Blue

Montezuma White Tequila

Montezuma Gold Tequila

Montezuma Triple Sec

Mr. Boston Cocktails

Mr. Boston Dark Rum

Mr. Boston Egg Nog

Mr. Boston Five Star Brandy

Mr. Boston Five Star Canadian

Mr. Boston Flavored Brandy

Mr. Boston Gin

Mr. Boston Light Rum

Mr. Boston Liqueurs

Mr. Boston Riva Gin

Mr. Boston Rock & Rye

Mr. Boston Schnapps

Mr. Boston Sour Apple Schnapps

Mr. Boston Screwdriver

Mr. Boston Vodka

Mr. Boston Whisky

Naked Jay Vodka

Northern Light Canadian

Old Pulteney Single Malt 12 Year Old

Old Pulteney Single Malt 17 Year Old

Old Pulteney Single Malt 21 Year Old

Old Thompson Blend

OLO Brazilian Silver Rum

OLO Brazilian Spiced Rum

Pikeman Gin

Pomegranate Spice

Purple Wave Vodka

Sabroso di Cafe Liqueur

Amaretto de Sabroso

Constellation Spirits

Schenley London Dry Gin

Schenley Reserve Whiskey

Schenley Rum

Schenley Vodka

Skol Gin

Skol Gold Rum

Skol Light Rum

Skol Vodka

Speyburn 10 Year Old Scotch

Speyburn Bradon Orach

Ten High Bourbon

Tom Moore Bourbon

Tom Moore Light Whiskey

Very Old Barton Bourbon

Villa Spinelli Asti Spumante

Wave Flavored Vodkas

Wide Eye Caffeinated Schnapps

Wide Eye Cherry Bomb

Wide Eye Mango Chill

Beam Global Spirits and Wine

Anis Castellana

Baker's

Basil Hayden

Booker's

Calvert Extra

Calvert Gin

Courvoisier VS

Courvoisier VSOP

Courvoisier XO

Courvoisier Cordon Bleu

Dekuyper Amaretto

Dekuyper Anisette

Dekuyper Apricot Brandy

Dekuyper Blue Curacao

Dekuyper Blackberry Brandy

Dekuyper Blueberry

Dekuyper Butterscotch Carmel

Dekuyper Cherry Brandy

Dekuyper Coconut

Dekuyper Cranberry

Dekuyper Crème de Banana

Dekuyper Crème de Cocoa Dark

Dekuyper Crème de Cocoa White

Dekuyper Crème de Menthe Green

Dekuyper Crème de Menthe White

Dekuyper Crème de Noya

Dekuyper Dry Orange

Dekuyper Green Curacao

Dekuyper Kiwi

Dekuyper Kwai Feh

Dekuyper Marasqin

Dekuyper Melon

Dekuyper Orange Curacao

Dekuyper Parfait Amour

Dekuyper Passion Fruit

Beam Global Spirits and Wine

Dekuyper Peach Tree	Kamchatka vodka
Dekuyper Pisang	Kamora
Dekuyper Pomegranate	Kessler
Dekuyper Raspberry	Knob Creek
Dekuyper Raspberry Pucker	Kullemerling
Dekuyper Red Apple	Laphroaig
Dekuyper Red Curacao	Larios Dry Gin
Dekuyper Red Orange	Lord Calvert
Dekuyper Sour Apple	Makers Mark
Dekuyper Sour Apple Pucker	Old Crow
Dekuyper Sour Grapefruit	Old Grandad
Dekuyper Sour Rhubarb	Old Overholt
Dekuyper Triple Sec	Ron Rico Rum
Dekuyper Tropical Mango	Sauza Blanco
Dekuyper Tropical Pineapple	Sauza Gold
Dekuyper Tropical Papaya	Sauza Hornitos
Dekuyper Watermelon	Sauza Conmemorativo
Dekuyper White Curacao	Sauza Tres Generaciones Plata
Dekuyper Wild Strawberry	Sourz Apple
Canadian Club	Starbucks Coffee Liqueur
DYC	Starbucks Cream Liqueur
El Tesoro	Tangle Ridge Canadian Whiskey
Fundador	Teacher's Scotch
Gibleys	Terry Centenario
Jim Beam	Vox Vodka
Jim Beam Black	Windsor Canadian
Jim Beam Small Batch	Wolfschmidt Vodka

Belvedere SA

Anises Berger

Anisette Marie Brizard

Belvedere Vodka

Belvedere Cytrus

Belvedere Pomarncza

Canadian's Tippers Whisky

Cortel Brandy

Gautier Cognac

Gautier Cognac Myriade Cru Reserve

Gautier Cognac Napoleon

Gautier Panatela Pineau des Chantres

Gautier Pinar del Rio Cognac XO

Gautier Traditional Rare Extra Vielle XO

Gautier VSOP

Gautier XO Gold and Blue

Jean Danflou Armagnac Exceptionnel

Jean Danflou Calvados

Jean Danflou Cognac

Jean Danflou Framboise

Jean Danflou Kirschwasser

Jean Danflou La Captive Calvados

Jean Danflou La Captive Poire Willaim

Glen Roger's Scotch

Litchao

Louis XV Brandy

Marie Brizard Amaretto

Marie Brizard Ananas

Marie Brizard Apricot Brandy

Marie Brizard Apry

Marie Brzard Blackberry

Marie Brizard Black Currant

Marie Brizard Blue Curacao

Marie Brizard Cherry Brandy

Marie Brizard Coconut

Marie Brizard Cranberry

Marie Brizard Crème de Banana

Marie Brizard Crème de Cacao Brown

Marie Brizard Crème de Cacao White

Marie Brizard Crème de Menthe Green

Marie Brizard Crème de Menthe White

Marie Brizard Grand Orange

Marie Brizard Limoncini

Marie Brizard Mangoa

Marie Brizard Mango Passion

Marie Brizard Mandarin

Marie Brizard Manzanita

Marie Brizard Melocoton

Marie Brizard Orange Curacao

Marie Brizard Parfait Amour

Marie Brizard Peach

Marie Brizard Pear William

Marie Brizard Raspberry

Marie Brizard Raspberry de Bordeux

Marie Brizard Strawberry

Belvedere SA

Marie Brizard Triple Sec

Marie Brizard Vanille de Madagascar

Marie Brizard Watermelon

Marie Brizard Wild Strawberry

Normandin Cognac

Old Lady's Gin

Pere Francios Calvados

Prince de Conde Armangac

San Jose Tequila

Sobieski Vodka

William Peel Whisky

Wisent Vodka

Bendistillery

Cascade Mountain Gin

Crater Lake Vodka

Crater Lake Hazelnut Espresso Vodka

Diamond 100 Vodka

Mazama Infused Pepper Vodka

Produced by Bendistillery (private labels)

Bu-TAY Premium Vodka

Bu-TAY Citrus Flavored Vodka

BU-TAY Ultra Premium Vodka

Desert Juniper Gin

Old Mill Rum

Berentze-Gruppe AG

Amaro Montenegro

Berentzen Apple

Berentzen Doppel Korn

Berentzen Edel Korn

Berentzen Green Pear

Berentzen Herber Zwetsch

Berentzen Hofkirsch

Berentzen Johann's Berry

Berentzen Plum

Berentzen Red Apple

Berentzen Sour Apple

Berentzen Traditions Korn

BerentzenWild Fruit

Bommerlunder Aquavit

Dirty Harry Lakritz-likor

Doornkat

Hansen Rum

Hansen President Rum

Hansen 54 Rum

Hansen White Rum

Limoncello Villa Massa

Linie Aquavit

Lufthansa Cocktail

Pushkin Black Star

Pushkin Red

Pushkin Time Warp

Pushkin Vodka

Pusser's Rum 42

Pusser's Rum 75

Strothman Weizen Korn

Vecchia Romagna Brandy

Vikingfjord Vodka

Bohemian Enterprises

Olivia Absinth

Boisett

Idol Vodka

Bols

Bokma

Bols Amaretto

Bols Apricot Brandy

Bols Bitter Orange

Bols Blackberry

Bols Blue

Bols Cherry Brandy

Bols Banana

Bols Butterscotch

Bols Coconut

Bols Coffee

Bols Corenwyn

Bols Creme de Cacao Brown

Bols Creme de Cacao

Bols Creme de Cassis

Bols Dry Orange

Bols Green Banana

Bols Green Tea

Bols Kirsch

Bols Kiwi Liqueur

Bols Lychee Liqueur

Bols Maraschino

Bols Mango

Bols Melon

Bols Parfait Amour

Bols Passion Fruit

Bols Peach

Bols Peppermint Green

Bols Peppermint White

Bols Rasberry (Framboise) Liqueur

Bols Pomegranate

Bols Red Orange

Bols Sloe Gin

Bols Strawberry (Fraise) Liqueur

Bols Triple Sec

Bols Vanilla Liqueur

Bols Vodka

Bols Vodka Forrest Fruits

Bols Vodka Lemon Ice

Bols Vodka Mandarin

Bols Vodka Peach

Bootz

Claeryn

Coebergh Classic

Coebergh Red Fruit

DAMRAK Amsterdam Gin

Els La Vera

Evita

Galliano Autentico

Galliano Balsamico

Bols

Galliano Ristretto

Galliano

Goldstrike

Hartevelt

Hoppe

Jonge Bols

Kontiki

Parade

Pisang Ambon

Pisang Ambon Guarana Lime

Vaccari Black

Vaccari Sambuca

Zeer Oude Bols

Zwart Fig

Bonidex Distillerie

Black Dee Vodka

Black Dee Whiskey

Holi Rose Liqueur

Imperial Diamond Brandy

Jack Williams Whiskey

Life Club Gin

Life Club Vodka

Maritel's Brandy

Mexicana Tequilliina

Silver Horse Vodka

Silver Horse Gin

Brown Forman

Canadian Mist

Chambord

Don Eduardo Tequila Silver

Don Eduardo Tequila Reposado

Don Eduardo Tequila Anejo

Early Times Bourbon

el Jimador Silver

el Jimador Reposado

el Jimador Anejo

Finlandia Classic

Finlandia Cranberry

Finlandia Grapefruit

Finlandia Lime

Finlandia Mango

Gentleman Jack

Herradura Silver

Herradura Reposado

Herradura Anejo

Jack Daniel's

Jack Daniel's Single Barrel

Old Forrester Bourbon

Pepe Lopez Tequila Siver

Pepe Lopez Tequila Gold

Southern Comfort

Stellar Gin

Tuaca

Woodford Reserve Kentucky Straight Bourbon

C & C Group

Carolans Irish Cream

Irish Mist

Frangelico

Tullamore Dew Irish Whisky

Campari

Aperol

Biancosarti

Cabo Wabo Blanco

Cabo Wabo Reposado

Cabo Wabo Anejo

Cabo Uno Ultra Luxury

Campari

Cinzano

Cynar

Diesus

Dreher

Drury's

Glen Grant

Mapo Mapo

Old Eight Whisky

Old Smuggler Whisky

Ouzo 12

Punch Barbieri Mandarin

Punch Barbieri Orange

Punch Barbieri Rum

Rum Des Antilles

SKYY Vodka

SKY Infusions Citrus

SKY Infusions Cherry

SKY Infusions Raspberry

SKY Infusions Grape

SKY Infusions Passion Fruit

X-Rated fusion liqueur

X-Rated Vodka

Jean-Marc XO Vodka

Zedda Piras

Castle Brands

Boru Vodka

Boru Vodka Crazzberry

Boru Vodka Citrus

Boru Vodka Orange

Brady's Irish Cream Liqueur

British Royal Navy Imperial Rum

Celtic Crossing Liqueur

Clontarf Irish Whiskey

Clontarf Single Malt Irish Whiskey

Gosling's Black Seal Rum

Gosling's Family Reserve Old Rum

Gosling's Gold Bermuda Rum

Knappogue Castle Irish Single Malt Whiskey

Jefferson's Bourbon

Jefferson's Reserve bourbon

Knappogue Castle 1951

Pallini Limoncello

Pallini Peachcello	Zlota Gorzka Vodka
Pallini Raspicello	Zubrowka Vodka
Sam Houston Bourbon	**Charles Jacquin et Cie., Inc.**
Sea Wynde Rum	Jacquin's Premium Blended Whiskey
Central European Distribution Corp	London Tower Gin
Absolwent Cranberry Vodka	Jacquin's Vodka Royale
Absolwent Gin	Jacquin's World Famous Rum (White and Gold)
Absolwent Lemon Vodka	
Absolwent Vodka	Bocador Rum (White and Gold)
Batory Vodka	Jacquin's French Napoleon Brandy
Boss Vodka	Jacquin's Five Star Brandy
Green Mark Vodka	Vendome VSOP Brandy
Niagra Vodka	Jacquin's Orange Gin
Old Pascus Blanco Rum	Jacquin's Cherry Vodka
Old Pascus Negro Rum	Jacquin's Lime Vodka
Ouzo Nostalagia	Jacquin's Apricot Brandy
Palace Vodka	Jacquin's Cherry Brandy
Parliament Black Currant Vodka	Jacquin's Coffee Brandy
Parliament Classic Vodka	Jacquin's Peach Brandy
Parliament Mandarin Vodka	Jacquin's Blackberry Brandy
Parliament Pepper Vodka	Jacquin's Ginger Brandy
Slaska Vodka	Jacquin's Amaretto
Soplica Cherry Vodka	Jacquin's Anisette
Soplica Staropolska Vodka	Jacquin's Banana Liqueur
Soplica Szlachetna Polska Vodka	Jacquin's Crème de Almond
Soplica Tradycyjna Polska Vodka	Jacquin's Crème de Cacao
Whiskream	Jacquin's Crème de Cassis
Zhuravia Vodka	Jacquin's Crème de Menthe

Charles Jacquin et Cie., Inc.

Jacquin's Grenadine

Jacquin's Kummel

Jacquin's Rock and Rye with Fruit

Jacquin's Sloe Gin

Jacquin's Crème de Strawberry

Jacquin's Triple Sec

Jacquin's Nirvana Banana Liqueur

Jacquin's Melon Liqueur

Jacquin's Peppermint Schnapps

Jacquin's Peach Schnapps

Jacquins's VSOP Five Star

Charles Medley Distillers

Wathens Single Barrel Bourbon

Chatham Imports

Baojing Bai Jiu

Baojing Vodka

Crop Organic Cucumber Vodka

Crop Organic Tomato Vodka

Crop Organic Vodka

Faretti Biscotti Famosi

Finian's Five

Marti Coco Suave

Marti Dorado Especial

Marti Mojito

Michter's 10 year-old Bourbon

Michter's 10 year-old Straight Rye

Michter's US 1 American Whiskey

Michter's US 1 Bourbon

Michter's US 1 Straight Rye

Primi Fruitti

Sambuca di Trevi

CL Worldwide Brands

1824 Rum

1919 Rum

Angostura Aromatic Bitters

Angostura Orange Bitters

Angostura 5 Year Old

Angostura 7 Year Old

Black Bottle

Bunnahabhain

Deanston

Hine Cognac

Hine VSOP

Ledaig

Scottish Leader

Tobemory

Diageo

Archers Peach

Archers Cranberry

Archers Lime

Bailey's

Bailey's Mint

Bailey's Caramel

Bell's 8 Year Old

Bell's Extra Special

Diageo

Bell's Special Reserve	Ciroc
Benmore	Crown Royal
Bertram's VO Brandy	Crown Royal Special Reserve
Black & White Scotch	Crown Royal XR
Black Haus	Dimple/ Pinch 12 Year Old
Buchanan's 12 year old	Dimple/ Pinch 15 Year Old
Buchanan's Special Reserve	Dimple/ Pinch 18 Year Old
Bulleit Bourbon	Don Julio Blanco
Bundaberg	Don Julio Reposado
Bundaberg OP	Don Julio Añejo
Bushmills Original	Don Julio 1942
Black Bush	Don Julio Real
Bushmills Malt 10 Year Old	Dulseda
Bushmills Malt 16 Year Old	George Dickel 12 year old
Bushmills Malt 21 Year Old	George Dickel Barrel Select
Cacique	Gilbey's Gin
Captain Morgan Original (Black label)	Godiva Original Chocolate
Captain Morgan Original Spiced Rum/ Gold	Godiva Milk Chocolate
Captain Morgan Silver Spiced	Godiva Mocha
Captain Morgan Private Stock	Godiva White Chocolate
Captain Morgan Parrot Bay Coconut	Goldschlager
Captain Morgan Parrot Bay Mango	Gordon's Gin
Captain Morgan Parrot Bay Pineapple	Gordon's Sloe Gin
Captain Morgan Parrot Bay Passion Fruit	Haig
Captain Morgan Tattoo Black Spiced Rum	J&B-6
Cardhu	J&B Jet
	J&B Nox
	J&B Rare

Diageo

J&B Reserve

Johnnie Walker Red Label

Johnnie Walker Black Label

Johnnie Walker Gold Label

Johnnie Walker Blue Label

Johnnie Walker Green Label

Johnnie Walker Swing

Don Julio Real

Dulseda

George Dickel 12 year old

George Dickel Barrel Select

Gilbey's Gin

Godiva Original Chocolate

Godiva Milk Chocolate

Godiva Mocha

Godiva White Chocolate

Goldschlager

Gordon's Gin

Gordon's Sloe Gin

Haig

J&B-6

J&B Jet

J&B Nox

J&B Rare

J&B Reserve

Johnnie Walker Red Label

Johnnie Walker Black Label

Johnnie Walker Gold Label

Johnnie Walker Blue Label

Johnnie Walker Green Label

Johnnie Walker Swing

Ketel One vodka

Ketel One Citron

Ketel One Jenever

Myers Rum

Grand Old Parr 12 year old

Old Parr 15 year old

Old Parr Superior 18 year old

Oronoco

Picon

Romana Sambuca

Rumple Minze

Safari

Seagram's 7 Crown

Seagram's VO

Singleton

Slate

Slate 20

Smirnoff Red

Smirnoff Blue

Smirnoff Black

Smirnoff Norsk

Smirnoff Black Cherry

Smirnoff Blueberry

Smirnoff Citrus

Diageo

Smirnoff Cranberry

Smirnoff Green Apple

Smirnoff Lime

Smirnoff Orange

Smirnoff Passion Fruit

Smirnoff Rasberry

Smirnoff Strawberry

Smirnoff Vanilla

Smirnoff Watermelon

Smirnoff White Grape

Spey Royal

Tanqueray Rangpur

Tanqueray 10

Tanqueray Sterling

The Real MacKenzie

Vat 69

White Horse

Windsor 12 year old

Windsor 17 year old

Distell Group

Amurula Cream

Angel's Share Cream

Collin's White Gold Brandy

Commando Brandy

Count Pushkin Vodka

Fish Eagle Brandy

Harrier Whisky

Klipdrift Gold

Klipdrift Premium

Knights Whisky

Mainstay Cane Spirit

Mellow Wood Brandy

Natchtmusik Chocolate

Nederburg Potstill Solera Brandy

Oude Meester Brandy

Oude Meester Brandy Reserve

Oude Meester Ginger

Oude Meester Peppermint

Richelieu Brandy

Romanoff Vodka

Seven Seas Cane Spirit

Three Ships Bourbon Cask

Three Ships Select Whisky

Three Ships 5 Year Old

Underberg Digestive

Van Ryn's 10 Year Old Brandy

Van Ryn's 12 Year Old Brandy

Van Ryn's 15 Year Old Brandy

Van Ryn's 20 Year Old Brandy

Viceroy Brandy

Dogfish Head Distilleries

Blue Hen Vodka

Dogfish Head Brown Honey Rum

Dogfish Head Jin

Dogfish Head Wit Spiced Rum

White Light Rum

Cask & Cream Caramel Temptation

Cask and Cream Chocolate Temptation

E. & J. Cask & Cream

E. & J. VS Brandy

E. & J. VSOP Brandy

Brugal Rum

Brugal Anejo Rum

Brugal Carta Dorada

Brugal Extra Viejo

Brugal Licor Unico

Brugal Ron Blanc

Brugal Siglo de Oro

Cutty Sark 12 year old

Cutty Sark 18 year old

Cutty Sark 25 year old

Cutty Sark Blended Whiskey

Cutty Sark Blended Malt Whiskey

Glenturret Single Malt

Glenturret 10 year old

Glenturret 14 year old

Glenturret 15 years old

Glenturret 29 years old

Highland Park 12

Highland Park 15

Highland Park 16

Highland Park 18

Highland Park 24

Highland Park 25

Highland Park 30

Tamdhu

The Famous Grouse

The Famous Grouse 10 year old

The Famous Grouse 12 year old

The Famous Grouse 15 year old

The Famous Grouse 18 year old

The Famous Grouse 21 year old

The Famous Grouse 30 year old

The Famous Grouse Bourbon Cask Finish

The Famous Grouse Cask Strength

The Famous Grouse Gold Reserve

The Famous Grouse Islay Finish

The Famous Grouse Liqueur

The Famous Grouse Port Wood Finish

The Famous Grouse Scottish Wood Finish

The Famous Grouse Vintage Malt 1987

The Famous Grouse Vintage Malt 1989

The Famous Grouse Vintage Malt 1990

The Famous Grouse Vintage Malt 1992

The Famous Grouse Wade Ceramic Highland Container

The Glenrothes 1975 Vintage

The Glenrothes 1978 Vintage

The Glenrothes 1985 Vintage

The Glenrothes 1991 Vintage

The Glenrothes 1994 Vintage

The Glenrothes 25 Year Old

The Glenrothes Select Reserve

The Macallan 1946

The Macallan 1948

The Macallan 1951

The Macallan 1961

The Macallan 50 Years Old

The Macallan Adami

The Macallan Blake

The Macallan Cask Strength

The Macallan Elegancia

The Macallan Exceptional I

The Macallan Exceptional II

The Macallan Exceptional III

Macallan Exceptional IV

The Macallan Exceptional V

The Macallan Exceptional VI

The Macallan Fine Oak series 8 years old

The Macallan Fine Oak series 10 years old

The Macallan Fine Oak series 12 years old

The Macallan Fine Oak series 15 years old

The Macallan Fine Oak series 17 years old

The Macallan Fine Oak series 18 years old

The Macallan Fine Oak series 21 years old

The Macallan Fine Oak series 25 years old

The Macallan Fine Oak series 30 years old

The Macallan Gran Reserva 1979

The Macallan Gran Reserva 1980

The Macallan Gran Reserva 1982

The Macallan Gran Reserva 2002

The Macallan Lalique

The Macallan Millennium

The Macallan Private Eye 1961

The Macallan Replica 1861

The Macallan Replica 1874

The Macallan Replica 1841

The Macallan Replica 1876

The Macallan Replica 1851

The Macallan Sherry Oak series 7 years old

The Macallan Sherry Oak series 10 years old

The Macallan Sherry Oak series 12 years old

The Macallan Sherry Oak series 18 years old

The Macallan Sherry Oak series 25 years old

The Macallan Sherry Oak series 30 years old

The Macallan Speaker Martin's

The Macallan Vintage Travel 20s

The Macallan Vintage Travel 30s

The Macallan Vintage Travel 40s

The Macallan Vintage Travel 50s

The Silver Grouse

The Snow Grouse

Foster's Group

Akropolis Oyzo

Barossa Brandy

Continental Advocaat

Continental Brown Crème de Cacao

Continental Cherry Advocaat

Continental Coconut

Continental Crème de Menthe

Continental Triple Sec

Continental White Crème de Cacao

Karlof

Kirov

Mildara

Prince Albert Gin

Roth Vodka

Ginebra San Miguel

Ginebra San Miguel

Ginebra San Miguel Blue

Ginebra San Miguel Premium Gin

Gran Matador Brandy

La Tondena Anejo Rum

La Tondena Anejo 5 year

La Tondena Dark Manila Rum

Tondena Gold Rum

Tondena White Rum

Grillos

Grillos Tequila Reposado

Grupo Cuervo S. A. de C. V.

José Cuervo Clásico Tequila

José Cuervo Especial Tequila

José Cuervo Black Medallio Tequila

José Cuervo Reserva de la Familia Tequila

José Cuervo Tradicional Tequila

José Cuervo Authentic Margarita

José Cuervo Golden Margarita

José Cuervo Citric Tequila

José Cuervo Oranjo Flavored Tequila

José Cuervo Tropina Flavored Tequila

José Cuervo Margarita Mix

Heaven Hill Distilleries

Água Luca Cachaça

Anderson Club Bourbon

Ansac Cognac VS

Ansac Cognac VSOP

Arandas Blanco Tequila

Arandas Oro Tequila

Aristocrat

Bernheim Original Straight Wheat Whiskey

Burnett's Gin

Burnett's Vodka

Burnett's Blueberry Vodka

Burnett's Cherry Vodka

Burnett's Citrus Vodka

Burnett's Coconut Vodka

Burnett's Cranberry Vodka

Heaven Hill Distilleries

Burnett's Grape Vodka

Burnett's Lime

Burnett's Mango

Burnett's Orange Vodka

Burnett's Peach Vodka

Burnett's Pomegranate Vodka

Burnett's Raspberry Vodka

Burnett's Sour Apple Vodka

Burnett's Strawberry Vodka

Burnett's Vanilla Vodka

Burnett's Watermelon Vodka

Cabin Still Bourbon

Christian Brothers Brandy VS

Christian Brothers VSOP

Christian Brothers XO

Christian Brothers Frost White bottlings

Christian Brothers Cream Sherry

Christian Brothers Dry Sherry

Christian Brothers Golden Sherry

Christian Brothers Meloso Cream Sherry

Christian Brothers Ruby Port

Christian Brothers Tawny Port

Cluny Scotch Whisky

Copa de Oro Coffee Liqueur

Coronet VSQ

Dixie Dew Corn Whiskey

Dubonnet Rouge

Dubonnet Blanc

Du Bouchett Balckberry Brandy

Du Bouchett Amaretto

Du Bouchett Apricot Brandy

Du Bouchett Blue Curaçao

Du Bouchett Butterscotch Schnapps Liqueur

Du Bouchett Cherry Brandy

Du Bouchett Cranberria liqueur

Du Bouchett Crème De Almond

Du Bouchett Crème De Banana

Du Bouchett Dark Cream De Cacao

Du Bouchett Green Cream De Menthe

Du Bouchett Hot Cinnamon Schnapps

Du Bouchett Melon Liqueur

Du Bouchett Orange Curacao

Du Bouchett Peach Brandy

Du Bouchett Peach Liqueur

Du Bouchett Peach Schnapps

Du Bouchett Peppermint Schnapps

Du Bouchett Root Beer Schnapps

Du Bouchett Sloe Gin

Du Bouchett Tangy Sour Apple Schnapps

Du Bouchett Tangy Sour Raspberry Schnapps

Du Bouchett Spicy Monster Schnapps

Du Bouchett Strawberry Liqueur

Du Bouchett Strawberry Schnapps

Heaven Hill Distilleries

Du Bouchett Triple Sec

Du Bouchett White Crème De Cacao

Du Bouchett White Crème De Menthe

Echo Spring Bourbon

Elijah Craig 12 year old

Elijah Craig Single Barrel 18 year old

Evan Williams Black Label

Evan Williams Single Barrel

Evan Williams Egg Nog

Evan Williams Master Distillers Select

Fighting Cock

Georgia Moon Corn Whiskey

Gukenheimer Whiskey

Harlequin Orange Liqueur

Heaven Hill Whiskey

Henry McKenna

Hpnotiq

J.T.S. Brown Bourbon

J.W. Corn Whiskey

J.W. Dant Bourbon

Kentucky Beau Whiskey

Kentucky Deluxe Bourbon

Kentucky Supreme Bourbon

La Certeza

Lazzaroni Amaretto

Lunazul

Mattingly & Moore Bourbon

Mellow Corn Whiskey

Old Fitzgerald

O'Mara's Irish Country Cream

Philadelphia Whiskey

Pikesville Supreme Rye Whiskey

Pama

Richelieu French Brandy

Rittenhouse Rye

Rittenhouse Bonded

Ron Llave Rum Blanco

Ron Llave Rum Oro

T.W. Samuels Bourbon

Vandermint Chocolate Liqueur

Whalers Big Island Banana

Whalers Great White

Whalers Killer Coconut

Whalers Original Dark Rum

Whalers Pineapple Paradise

Whalers Spiced Rum

Whalers Reserve Dark Rum

Whalers Vanilla Rum

Wilson Whiskey

High West Distillers

Rocky Mountain Rye 21 Year Old

Rocky Mountain Rye 16 Year Old

Rendezvous Rye Whiskey

Vodka 7000

Highwood Distillers

Abstract Amaretto Liqueur

Abstract Apricot Brandy

Abstract Blue Curacao

Abstract Crème de Cacao

Abstract Crème de Banane

Abstract Melon Liqueur

Abstract Peach Schnapps

Abstract Sambuca

Bullets Assorted

Bullets Raspberry Sour

Bullets Grape Sour

Bullets Irish Cream

Bullets Strawberry Tequila

Bullets Rootbeer

Bullets Blue Sambuca

Bullets Tequila

Ceili Irish Cream

Centennial 10 Year Old Rye

Century Reserve Canadian Rye Whisky 21 Year Old

Century Reserve 15-20 Year Old Special Blend

Colita Coffee del Sol

Cortez Gold Tequila

Dublin Irish Cream

El Conquistador Blanco Tequila

Empire Gin

Graffitti Amaretto

Graffitti Blue Curacao

Graffitti Butterscotch Schnapps

Graffitti Crème de Banane

Graffitti Crème de Cacao

Graffitti Melon

Graffitti Peach Schnapps

Graffitti Rootbeer Schnapps

Graffitti Triple Sec

Highwood Black Russian

Highwood China White Crème de Cacao

Highwood Imported White Rum

Highwood Triple Sec

Highwood Pure Canadian Vodka

Highwood Pure Canadian Rye Whisky

Marushka Vodka

Long Island Iced Tea

Longshotz Assorted

Longshotz Virtual X'Tacy

Longshotz Wet-N-Juicey

Longshotz Body Buzz

Longshotz Wild Rose Cream

Longshotz Fuzzy Navel

Longshotz NRG Infused Vodka

MacClellands Scotch Whiskey

Midnight Blue Sambucca

Highwood Distillers

Momento Amber Rum

Parkland Vodka

Potter's Black Russian

Potter's London Dry Gin

Potter's Traditional Dark Navy Rum

Potter's Long Island Iced Tea

Potter's Margarita Mix

Potter's White Rum

Potter's Special Old Rye Whisky

Potter's Premium Vodka

Pristina Vodka

Quartermater's Canadian Rye Whisky

Rangeland Rum

Sahara Dry Gin

Saskatchewan Parkland Vodka

Saskatchewan Rangeland Rum

Saskatchewan Wheatland Rye Whisky

Saskatoon Berry Liqueur

Sourwave Grape Liqueur

Sourwave Raspberry Liqueur

Sweet Sippin Maple Whisky

Wheatland Rye Whisky

White Lightning Vodka

White Sands Rum

Wild Rose Cream

Wild Caramel Toffee Cream

Wild Fire Cinnamon Whisky

Hite Brewery Co.

Chun Kook

Elvan Soju

HITE Soju

ILPUM Jinro

Jinro Chamjinisulro Soju

Jinro Chamisul Fresh Soju

Jinro Gold Soju

Jinro Soju

Juniper

Kingdom 12 Year Old

Kingdom 17 Year Old

Kingdom 21 Year Old

Lancelot 12 Year Old

Lancelot 17 Year Old

Lancelot 21 Year Old

Lancelot 30 Year Old

Mae Haw Soo

Yethang

Hood River Distilleries

Brokers Gin

Cockspur Rum

Cockspur 12 year old Rum

HRD Peach Schnapps

HRD Rootbeer Schnapps

HRD Vodka

Knickers Irish Cream

Monarch Brandy

Hood River Distilleries

Monarch Gin

Monarch Peach Schnapps

Monarch Peppermint Schnapps

Monarch Rum

Monarch Tequila

Monarch Triple Sec

Monarch Vodka

Pendelton Whiskey

Spudka Vodka

Ullr Schapps

Yazi Ginger Vodka

Iceberg Vodka

Iceberg Vodka

Iceberg Gin

Iceberg Water

Iceberg Silver Rum

Iceberg Gold Rum

Infinium Spirits

Bafferts Gin

Bafferts Mint

Branca Menta

Casa Noble Anejo

Casa Noble Blanco

Casa Noble Reposado

Corralejo Tequila Anejo

Corralejo Tequila Reposado

Corralejo Tequila Triple Distilled

Crystal Head Vodka

Fernet Branca

Seagrams Extra Smooth Vodka

Seagrams Apple Vodka

Seagrams Blackberry Vodka

Seagrams Citrus Vodka

Seagrams Expresso Vodka

Seagrams Platinum Select Vodka

Seagrams Raspberry Vodka

Seagrams Wild Grape Vodka

Templeton Rye

The Last Drop - Scotch Whisky

Zaya 12 yo Rum

Innovative Liquors

267 Rum Infusion Mango

267 Rum Infusion Wild Berry

267 Tequila Infusion Chili Pepper

267 Vodka Infusion Cranberry

267 Vodka Infusion Olive and Pearl Onion

Kirin Brewery Co Ltd

Four Roses Black Label Bourbon

Four Roses Platinum Bourbon

Four Roses Single Barrel 86

Four Roses Single Barrel 100

Four Roses Small Batch 90

Four Roses Yellow Label Bourbon

Inner Circle Rum

Mckenna Bourbon

Kobrand Corp

Alizé Blue

Alizé Cognac VS

Alizé Congnac VSOP

Alizé Gold Passion

Alizé Red Passion

Alizé Rose

Alizé Wild Passion

Appleton Estate 21 year old

Appleton Estate Extra 12 year old

Appleton Estate V/X

Appleton Estate Reserve

Appleton Jamaica Special Rum

Appleton Jamaica White Rum

Café Bohême Coffee Crème Liqueur

Coruba Jamaica Dark Rum

Delamain Extra

Delamain Grand Champagne Cognac XO

Delamain Le Voyage

Delamain Reserve de la Famille

Delamain Tres Venerable

Delamain Vesper

Delamain Vintage

Depaz Blue Cane Amber Rhum

Guyot Creme de Cassis

Larressingle Armagnac Vintage

Larressingle Armagnac VSOP

Larressingle Armagnac XO

J. Wray and Nephew White Overproof Rum

Larressingle Armagnac XO

Larressingle Armagnac Vintage

Laird and Company

Bankers Club Blended Whisky

Bankers Club French Brandy

Bankers Club Gin

Bankers Club Gold Rum

Bankers Club Rum

Bankers Club Scotch

Bankers Club Vodka

Canadian Gold

Casoni Limoncello Di Sorrento

Dunheath Scotch

Five O' Clock Blended Whisky

Five O' Clock Bourbon

Five O' Clock French Brandy

Five O' Clock Gin

Five O' Clock Imported Rum

Five O' Clock Imported Gold Rum

Five O' Clock Apple Mist Vodka

Five O' Clock Vodka

G & W Private Stock Bourbon

Kasser's Blended Whisky

Kasser's Gin

Kasser's Vodka 80

Kasser's Vodka 100

Laird and Company

Lairds Apple Jack

Lairds Captain Apple Jack

Lairds Apple Brandy 100

Lairds Captain Apple Jack

Lairds Rare Apple Brandy (12 Year Old)

Lairds Old Apple Brandy (7 1/2 Year Old)

Lairds Gin 80

Lairds Gin 100

Lairds Rum

Lairds Vodka

Mazzetti Grappa Di Arneis

Mazzetti Grappa Di Barbera

Mazzetti Grappa Di Moscato

Mazzetti Grappa Di Nebbliolo

Mazzetti Intesa

Moletto Grappa Di Arneis

Moletto Grappa Di Barbera

Moletto Grappa Di Moscato

Moletto Grappa Di Nebblio

Moletto Distillato D'Uva

Peachka Vodka

Regency Di Vinci Amaretto

Senators Club Blended Whisky

Senators Club French Brandy

Senators Club Gin

Senators Club Gold Rum

Senators Club White Rum

Senators Club Vodka

Senators Club Spiced Rum

Seven Star Blended Whiskey

Sortilege Maple Syrup

Uvix Vodka

William Penn Blended Whisky

Zapata Tequila Gold

Zapata Tequila Silver

Zapata Triple Sec

La Martiniquaise

Anee Calvados

Anis Gras

Bally Rum

Busnel Calvados

Courcel Cognac

Daure

Dillon Rum

Ducastaing Armagnac

Floranis

Gibson's Gin

Glen Turner Whisky

Label 5 Whiskey

Negrita Rum

Old Nick

Old Virginia

Olympio

Porto Cruz

Poliakov Vodka

Sam Barton Whiskey

St. James Rum

St. Vivant

Sylvain Calvados

Maine Distilleries

Cold River Potato Vodka

Mast-Jaegermeister

Jaegermeister

Schlehenfeuer

McCormick's Distilleries

360 Vodka

Cambridge Gin

Congress Gin

Canadian Woods

Hussongs Anejo

Hussongs Reposado

KeKe Beach

McCormick's Blended Scotch Whisky

McCormick's Brandy

McCormick's American Blended Whiskey

McCormick's Canadian Whisky

McCormick's Citrus Vodka

McCormick's Old Style Whisky

McCormick's Gin

McCormick's Gold Label Straight Bourbon

McCormick's Irish Cream

McCormick's Rums

McCormick's Tequilas

McCormick's Triple Sec Liqueur

McCormick's Vodka

McCormick's Apple Vodka

McCormick's Orange Vodka

McCormick's Peach Vodka

McCormick's Raspberry Vodka

McCormick's Vanilla Vodka

McClomick's Watermelon Vodka

Montego Bay Gold Rum

Montego Bay Silver Rum

Rio Grande Triple Se

Ron Rio Gold Rum

Ron Rio Silver Rum

Pancho Villa Gold Tequila

Pancho Villa Silver Tequila

Platte Valley KY Corn Whiskey

Stillbrook Blend

Stillbrook Old KY Whiskey

Tarantula Azul

Tarantula Banana Colada

Tarantula Lime

Tarantula Orange

Tarantula Strawberry

Tarantula Plata

Tarantula Reposado

Tequila Rose

Tequila Rose Cocoa

Tequila Rose Java

Viaka Vodka

Moet-Hennessy

10 Cane Rum

Ardberg Malt Whiskey

Armagnac LaPostolle

Cherry Marnier

Wen Jun Bai Jiu

Cognac Marnier VS

Cognac Marnier VSOP

Cognac Marnier XO

Glen Moray Whisky 12 Years Old

Glen Moray Whisky 16 Years Old

Glen Moray whisky Special Edition Classic

Glen Moray whisky 1962 Distillery Manager's Choice

Glen Moray whisky 20 Years Old

Glen Moray whisky 30 Years Old

1963 Glen Moray

1964 Glen Moray

1984 Glen Moray

1989 Glen Moray

1991 Mountain Oak Malt

Glenmorangie Whisky

Glenmorangie Nectar D'or

Lasanta

Glenmorangie Quinta Ruban

Glenmorangie 18 year old

Glenmorangie 25 year old

Grand Marnier Cordon Rouge

Grand Marnier Cuvee du Cent Cinquantenaire

Grand Marnier Cuvee du Centenaire

Grand Marnier Louis Alexandre

Hennessy VS

Hennessy Privilege VSOP

Hennessy XO

Hennessy Paradis Extra

Richard Hennessy

Hennessy Ellipse

Navan

Pineau Des Charentes Marnier

Monin Spirits

Monin Apricot

Monin Banana

Monin Blackberry

Monin Blue Curaçao

Monin Cassis de Dijon

Monin Coffee

Monin Cherry Brandy

Monin Dark Cocoa

Monin Frosted Mint

Monin Green Apple

Monin Green Mint

Monin Orange Curaçao

Monin Peach

Monin Raspberry

Monin Strawberry

Monin Tangerine	Nemirovskaya Osobaya
Monin Triple Sec Curaçao	**Niche**
Monin Vanilla	Cachaca Samba Brasil
Monin Violet	Calvados Cardinal
Monin Watermelon	Calvados Coquerel VSOP
Monin White Cocoa	Calvados Pomme D'Eve
Monin Wild Strawberry	Carlsbader Becherovka
Mozart Distilleries	Cognac Francet
Mozart Chocorange	Costa del Sole Limoncello
Mozart Dark	Der Lachs "Original" Goldwasser
Mozart Original	Doornkaat German Schnapps
Mozart White	Dujardin VSOP
Nemiroff	Fassbind Eau De Vie
Lex Vodka	Echte Kroatzbeere Blackberry
Nemiroff Cranberry Vodka	Bismarck Doppelkorn
Nemiroff Honey Pepper Vodka	Grappa Cividina
Nemiroff Lemon Vodka	Illy Espresso Liqueur
Nemiroff Light Vodka	Kammer Blackforest Kirschwasser
Nemiroff Original Vodka	Kammer Williams "Pear in a Bottle"
Nemiroff Premium Currant Vodka	Killepitsch Premium Kraeuter
Nemiroff Premium De Luxe Vodka	Laine Napoleon Brandy
Nemiroff Premium Lime Vodka	Navip Slivovitz
Nemiroff Strong Vodka	Schwarzwalder Kirschwasser
Nemiroff Ukrainian Birch Special	Sempé Armagnac
Nemiroff Ukrainian Rye Honey	Schladerer Edelkirsch Liqueur
Nemiroff Ukrainian Rye Selected	Schladerer Himbeergeist
Nemiroff Ukrainian Wheat Selected	Schlichte Steinhaeger Dry Gin
Nemirovskaya	Schoenauer Appel Schnapps

Stroh Jagertee

Stroh Obstler

Stroh 80

Teton Glacier Potato Vodka

Verpoorten Advocaat

Helbing Kuemmel

Nolet Spirits

Ketel One Citron

Ketel One Vodka

Orchid Liqueurs

Guava Liqueur

Lychee Liqueur

Mango Liqueur

Passion Fruit Liqueur

Pomegranate

Osborne Grupo

103 Blanco Sherry Brand

103 Negra Sherry Brandy

Alma de Magno Sherry Brandy

Anis Del Mono Dulce

Alma de Magno Sherry Brandy

Conde de Osborne Sherry Brandy

Independeca Sherry Brandy

Magno Sherry Brandy

Ponche Santa Maria

Tovaritch Vodka

Veterano Sherry Brandy

Xantiamen Agardierre Oruju

Xantiamen Licor de Herbes

Paramount Liquors

Black Duck Cranberry Liqueur

Canadian Bay

Colonial Club Liqueurs

Gertide Kummel

Glaros Ouzo

Grand Muriel Orange Liqueur

Karimba Coffee Liqueur

Korski Vodka

Lady Bligh Spiced Rum

Lady Bligh Coconut Rum

La Salle Cordials

Paramount Gin

Paramount Vodka

Paramount Rum

Paramount flavored Vodkas

Paramount Cordials

LaPrima Tequila

Rock and Rye

Partida Tequila

Añejo

Blanco

Extra Añejo Elegante

Reposado

Patron Spirits Company

Gran Patron

Patron Anejo

Patron Spirits Company

Patron Burdeos

Patron Citronge

Patron Reposado

Patron Silver

Patron XO Cafe

Pyrat Cask

Pyrat XO Reserve

Ultimat Vodka

Peach Street Distillers

Colorado Straight Bourbon

Goat Artisan Vodka

Goat Peach Vodka

Grappa of Viognier

Gewurztraminer Grappa

Jackalope Gin

Jack and Jenny Kirsch Eau de Vie

Jack and Jenny Peach Eau de Vie

Jenny and Jack Pear Eau de Vie

Jenny and Jack Plum Eau de Vie

Peach Brandy

Viognier Grappa

Pernod Ricard

100 Pipers Scotch

Altai

Amaro Ramazzotti

Anejo Los Reyes Brandy

Ararat Brandy

Azteca De Oro Brandy

Ballantines' Finest

Ballantine's 12 Year Old

Ballantine's 17 Year Old

Ballantine's 21 Year Old

Ballantine's 30 Year Old

Beefeater Gin

Becherovka

Bisquit Cognac

Blenders Pride Whisky

Brandy Domecq

Chivas 12 Year Old

Chivas Regal 18 Gold Signature

Chivas Regal Royal Salute

Chivas Regal 25 Year Old Scotch Whisky

Clan Campbell

Cork Dry Gin

Cusenier

Dita

Doble V Whiskey

Don Pedro Brandy

Dunbar Whisky

Fernet Capri

Havana Club Añejo Blanco

Havana Club Añejo 3 Años

Havana Club Añejo Especial

Havana Club Añejo 7 Años

Havana Club Añejo Reserva

Pernod Ricard

Havana Club Cuban Barrel Proof
Havana Club Máximo Extra Añejo
Hiram Walker Apricot Brandy
Hiram Walker Blackberry Brandy
Hiram Walker Cherry Brandy
Hiram Walker Coffee Brandy
Hiram Walker Ginger Brandy
Hiram Walker Peach Brandy
Hiram Walker Amaretto
Hiram Walker Amaretto & Cognac
Hiram Walker Anisette
Hiram Walker Black Raspberry
Walker Crème de Banana
Hiram Walker Crème de Cacao Brown
Hiram Walker Crème de Cacao White
Hiram Walker Crème de Cassis
Hiram Walker Crème de Menthe Green
Hiram Walker Crème de Menthe White
Hiram Walker Crème de Noyaux
Hiram Walker Crème de Strawberry
Hiram Walker Hazelnut
Hiram Walker Kirschwasser
Hiram Walker Melon Liqueur
Hiram Walker Orange Curacao
Hiram Walker Sambuca
Hiram Walker Sloe Gin
Hiram Walker Triple Sec
Hiram Walker Butterscotch Schnapps
Hiram Walker Cinnamon Schnapps
Hiram Walker Mango Schnapps
Hiram Walker Peach Schnapps
Hiram Walker Pear Schnapps
Hiram Walker Peppermint Schnapps
Hiram Walker Pink Grapefruit Schnapps
Hiram Walker Pomegranate Schnapps
Hiram Walker Pumpkin Spice Schnapps
Hiram Walker Raspberry Schnapps
Hiram Walker Rootbeer Schnapps
Hiram Walker Sour Apple Schnapps
Hiram Walker Tangerine Schnapps
Huzzar, Imperial Scotch
Jameson
Jameson 12 Year Old
Jameson 18 Year Old
Jameson Gold Reserve
Jameson Rarest Vintage Reserve
Janeiro Cachaça
Kahlúa
Kahlúa Especial
Kahlúa French Vanilla
Kahlúa Hazelnut
Kahlúa Mocha
Lodowa
Long John Scotch
Longmorn Single malt

Pernod Ricard

Malibu Coconut

Malibu Mango

Malibu Passion Fruit

Malibu Pineapple

Malibu Tropical Banana

Martell V.S.

Martell V.S.O.P.

Martell Cordon Bleu

Martell L'Or, Martell X.O, Martell Noblige, Martell L'Art, Martell Création

Montilla

Natu Nobilis Whisky

Olmeca Anejo Tequila

Olmeca Blanco Tequila

Olmeca Gold Tequila

Olmeca Reposado Tequila

Passport Scotch

Paddy Irish Whiskey

Pastis 51

Pernod

Pernod with absinthe extract

Polar Ice

Powers Irish Whiskey

Presidente Brandy

Renault Cognac

Ricard

Royal Stag Whisky

Ruavieja

Russell's Reserve Rye

Sao Francisco Cachaça

Scapa Single Malt

Seagram's Distiller's Reserve

Seagram's Gin

Soho

Strathisla Single malt

Suze

The Glenlivet 12 Year Old

The Glenlivet 15 Year Old

The Glenlivet 18 Year Old

The Glenlivet Archive 21 Year Old

The Glenlivet Cellar Collection

The Glenlivet Nàdurra

The Glenlivet 25 Year Old

Tia Maria

Tormore Single malt

Viuda de Romero Tequila

Walker Special Old Canadian

Wild Turkey American Honey

Wild Turkey 80

Wild Turke 86.8

Wild Turkey 101

Wild Turkey Rare Breed

Wild Turkey Russell's Reserve

Wild Turkey Kentucky Spirit

Wisers Canadian

Wyborowa	**Remy - Cointreau**
Zoco	Cognac Rémy Martin
Zubrowka	Cointreau
Piedmont Distiller's Inc	Izzara
Catdaddy Carolina Moonshine	L'Age D'Or de Rémy Martin
Midnite Moon Moonshine	Louis XIII de Rémy Martin
Pierre Guy Distillerie	Metaxa
Absinthe Francois Guy	Mt. Gay Rum
Anisette	Passao
Bacchus Ciane	Ponche Kuba
Ciane	Rémy Martin Grand Cru
Crème de Casis de Dijon	Rémy Martin VSOP
Fruit Souffle	Rémy Martin Club
Guignorix	Rémy Martin 1738 Accord Royal
Le Vert Sapin	Rémy Martin XO Spécial
Peche de Vigne	St. Remy
Pontarlier - Anis Sec 45%	Rémy Martin XO Excellence
Pontarlier - Anis Sec 45% A L'Ancienne (No Sugar)	Rémy Martin Extra
Satinees Cordials	Rémy Red
Siranis	Rémy Silver
p.i.n.k. Spirits	St Rémy
p.i.n.k. Gin	**Sazerac Company**
p.i.n.k. Rum	Amaretto di Padrino
p.i.n.k. Tequila	Ancient Age Bourbon
p.i.n.k. Sake	Blanton's Single-Barrel
p.i.n.k. Vodka	Buffalo Trace Bourbon
p.i.n.k. White Whiskey	Canadian Hunter Canadian Whisky
	Carstairs

Sazerac Company

Crown Russe Gin

Crown Russe Vodka

Diesel Natural

Dobra Vodka

Denaka Vodka

Denaka Vanilla Vodka

Denaka Raspberry Vodka

Denaka Citron Vodka

Denaka Orange Vodka

Denaka Grape Vodka

Denaka Black Cherry Vodka

Dobra Vodka

Dr. McGillicuddy's Mentholmint Schnapps

Dr. McGillicuddy's Vanilla Schnapps

Dr. McGillicuddy's Cherry Schnapps

Dr. McGillicuddy's Lemon Drop Schnapps

Fireball Cinnamon Whisky

Eagle Rare Single-Barrel 10-year-old Bourbon

Eagle Rare 17 years old

Elmer T. Lee Bourbon

Feeney's Irish Cream Liqueur

Hancock's Reserve Single-Barrel Bourbon

Glenfarclas Scotch

Herbsaint Liqueur d'Anis

James Foxe Whisky

John Handy Scotch

Benchmark Bourbon

Legacy Whisky

Kentucky Dale Whisky Legendre

Miles Gin

Mims Gin

Mims Vodka

Mint Gin

Nikolai Gin

Nikolai Vodka

Peychaud's Bitters

Praline Liqueur

P-51 Cachaca

Rain Vodka

Rich & Rare Canadian Whisky

Rock Hill Farms Single-Barrel Bourbon

Ron Pontalba Rum

Royal Canadian Canadian Whisky

Sazerac Rye 18 Years Old

Sir Malcolm Scotch

Taaka Gin

Taaka Platinum Vodka

Taaka Vodka

Tijuana Tequila

Tina Tequila

Torada Tequila

Torada Triple Sec

Van Winkle Family Reserve Bourbon

W.L. Weller Bourbon

Sichuan Swellfun

Shui Jing Fang Classic Bai Jiu

Shui Jing Fang Wellbay Bai Jiu

South Pacific Distilleries

Roaring Forties Apple Schnapps

Roaring Forties Dry Gin

Roaring Forties Gin

Roaring Forties Oak Aged Dark Rum

Roaring Forties Oak aged Overproof Amber Rum Single Cask 6 -7 Years Old

Roaring Forties Rum

Roaring Forties Peach Schnapps

Roaring Forties Vodka

St. George Spirits (Hanger One)

Aqua Perfecta Framboise Eau de Vie

Aqua Perfecta Framboise Liqueur

Aqua Perfecta Grappa of Zinfandel

Aqua Perfecta Kirsch Eau de Vie

Aqua Perfecta Pear Liqueur

Aqua Perfecta Poire Eau de Vie

Hangar One Straight Vodka

Hangar One Buddah's Hand Citron

Hangar One Kaffir Lime

Hangar One Mandarin Blossom

Hangar One Fraser River Raspberry

St. George Single Malt Whiskey

St. George Absinthe Verte

Strega Alberti Benevento SpA

Grappa Bianca

Grappa di Aglianico

Strega Cream

Grappa di Falanghina

Limoncello di Sorrento

Liquore Strega

Strega Cream

Strega Riserva

Suntory

MIDORI Melon Liqueur

The Blue Blue Curacao

Creme de Kyoho "Murasaki"

Fruit Liqueur "Miss Peach"

Square Cassis

Square Litchi

Square Peach

Square Mascut

Square Pineapple

Japonais "Maccha"

Japonais "Sakura"

Japonais "Koubai"

Hermes Orange curacao

Hermes White curacao

Hermes Blue curacao

Hermes Apricot brandy

Hermes Violet

Hermes Cherry brandy

Suntory

Hermes Cacao

Hermes Green Tea

Hermes Peppermint

Hermes White peppermint

Hermes Moka

Hermes Strawberry

Hermes Banana

Hermes Melon

Lejay Crème de Cassis

Lejay Le Double Cassis

Lhote Crème de Cassis

Lejay Crème de Framboise

Lejay Crème de Blueberry

Lejay Crème Quartet

Lejay Crème de Peche

Lejay Crème de Apricot

Lejay Crème de Strawberry

Lejay Green Apple

Lejay Peach

Paraiso Litchi

Passimo Passion Fruit Liqueur

Cocomo Coconut Liqueur

Mangoyan Mango Liqueur

Biscota Cookie & Cream Liqueur

Lazool Grapefruit Liqueur

Suntory Ice Gin

Suntory Dry Gin Extra

Suntory Dry Gin Smooth

Suntory Brandy X.O Super Deluxe

Suntory Brandy X.O Deluxe

Suntory Brandy X.O Silky

Suntory Brandy X.O Slim Bottle

Suntory Brandy V.S.O.P

Suntory Brandy V.S.O.P Frosty Bottle

Suntory Brandy V.S.O.P Slim Bottle

Suntory Brandy V.S.O.P Silky

Suntory Brandy V.S.O

Suntory Brandy V.P

Suntory Whisky HIBIKI 21 Years

Suntory Whisky HIBIKI GOLD LABEL

Suntory Whisky HIBIKI 17 Years

Suntory Whisky HIBIKI 50.5

Suntory Whisky Imperial

Suntory Single Malt Whisky YAMAZAKI 25 Years

Suntory Single Malt Whisky YAMAZAKI 18 Years

Suntory Single Malt Whisky YAMAZAKI 12 Years

Suntory Single Malt Whisky YAMAZAKI 10 Years

Suntory Single Malt Whisky HAKUSHU 18 Years

Suntory Single Malt Whisky HAKUSHU 12 Years

Suntory Single Malt Whisky HAKUSHU 10 Years

"A woman drove me to drink, and I'll be a son of a gun, but I never even wrote to thank her."

- W.C. Fields, 20th Century Actor / Humorist

Suntory

Suntory Single Malt Whisky Yamazaki Distillery Cask Strength 15 Years

Suntory Single Malt Whisky Hakushu Distillery Cask Strength 15 Years

Suntory Whisky ROYAL 15 Years Gold Label

Suntory Whisky ROYAL PREMIUM 15 Years

Suntory Whisky ROYAL PREMIUM 15 Years Slim Bottle

Suntory Whisky ROYAL 12 Years

Suntory Whisky ROYAL 12 Years Slim Bottle

Suntory Pure Malt Whisky HOKUTO 12 Years

Suntory Whisky HOKUTO 50.5

Suntory Whisky RESERVE 10 Years

Suntory Whisky RESERVE 10 Years Sherry Oak

Suntory Whisky OLD 43°

The Suntory OLD

Suntory Whisky KAKUBIN

Suntory Whisky SHIROKAKU

Suntory Whisky AJIWAI KAKUBIN

Suntory Whisky ZEN

Suntory Whisky ZENMARU

Suntory Whisky WHITE

Suntory Whisky Red

Torys Whisky Square

Torys Whisky

Torys Whisky Black

Tanduay Distillers

Barcelona Brandy

Cossack Vodka

London Dry Gin

Tanduay Rum 1854

Tanduay 5 years

Tanduay Centennnial Rhum

Tanduay E.S.Q.

Tanduay Philippine Rhum

Tanduay Primiero Ron 8 Anos

Tanduay Rhum 65

Tanduay Superior

Tanduay White

Thai Beverage

Blend 285

Blue

Crown 99

Hong Thong

Mangkorn Thong

Mekhong Traditional Thai Spirit

Mekhong Superior

Niyomthai White Spirit

Phai Thong White Spirit

Ruang Kao White Spirit

Sangsom Premium

Sangsom Similan

Sangsom Superior

Siang Chun

Sua Dum

White Tiger White Spirit

Three-D Spirits Inc
Jolly Roger Silver Rum

RedRum

Vodoo Spiced Rum

Tito's
Tito's Handmade Vodka

Tukys Flavored Tequila
Tukys Coffee Tequila

Tukys Lime Tequila

Tukys Mandarin Orange Tequila

Tukys Strawberry Tequila

Tukys Watermelon Tequila

United Spirits (United Breweries)
Alcazar

Bagpiper Whisky

Blue Riband Gin

Black Dog Whisky

Caesar Brandy

Celebration XXX Rum

Dalmore Single Malt

Director's Special Whisky

Fettercairn Single Malt

Glayva liqueur

Honey Bee Brandy

Isle of Jura Single Malt

John Exshaw Brandy

McDowell's No.1 Whisky

McDowell's No.1 Brandy

McDowell's Celebration Rum

Old Cask Rum

Red Riband Vodka

Romanov

Signature

Vladivar Vodka

White Mischief

Whyte & Mackay Blended Scotch Whiskies

Van Gogh Spirits
Van Gogh Acai - Blueberry Vodka

Van Gogh Banana Vodka

Van Gogh Black Cherry Vodka

Van Gogh Citroen Vodka

Van Gogh Classic 80-proof Vodka

Van Gogh Coconut Vodka

Van Gogh Double Espresso

Van Gogh Dutch Chocolate Vodka

Van Gogh Espresso Vodka

Van Gogh Gin

Van Gogh Mango Vodka

Van Gogh Melon Vodka

Van Gogh Mojito Mint Vodka

Van Gogh Oranje Vodka

Van Gogh Pineapple Vodka

Van Gogh Pomegranate Vodka

Van Gogh Raspberry Vodka

Van Gogh Vanilla Vodka

Wild Appel Vodka

Vin and Spirits

Absolut VODKA Absolut	Cruzan Coconut
Absolut Peppar	Cruzan Guava
Absolut Citron	Cruzan Mango
Absolut Kurant	Cruzan Pineapple
Absolut Mandrin	Cruzan Rasberry
Absolut Vanilia	Cruzan Vanilla
Absolut Raspberri	MINTTU 40%
Absolut Apeach	MINTTU 50%
Absolut Ruby Red	MINTTU Black
Absolut Pears	Plymouth Gin 41.2%
Absolut Mango	Plymouth Gin Navy Strength 57%
Absolut 100	Plymouth Sloe Gin
Level Vodka	Plymouth Gin Fruit Cup
Fris Vodka	Malteser Bitter
Fris Apple vodka	Nordso Bitter
Fris Lime vodka	Gammel Dansk Bitter Dram
Luksusowa Vodka	Gammel Bitter Citrus Dram
Luksusowa Vodka 40%	Champion Bitter
Luksusowa Vodka 50%	Carillo Bitter
Luksusowa Vodka Traditional Honey	Plymouth Gin 41.2%
Cruzan 151 Proof Rum	Plymouth Gin Navy Strength 57%
Cruzan Aged Light Rum	Plymouth Sloe Gin
Cruzan Aged Dark Rum	Plymouth Gin Fruit Cup
Cruzan Single Barrel Rum	
Cruzan Banana	
Cruzan Black Cherry	
Cruzan Citrus	

**Come, fill the cup to keep the spirits up,
By drinking the spirits down.**

- Toast - Anonymous

White Rock Distilleries

Adams Private Stock Whiskey

Aunt Bea's Butterscotch Liqueur

Baja Banana Tequila & Cream Liqueur

Baja Del Rio Tequila & Cream Liqueur

Baja Cherry Tequila & Cream Liqueur

Baja Grape Tequila & Cream Liqueur

Baja Mango Tequila & Cream Liqueur

Baja Mocha Tequila & Cream Liqueur

Baja Tango Tequila & Cream Liqueur

Baja Rosa Tequila & Cream Liqueur

Barbarossa Banana Rum

Barbarossa Cherry Rum

Barbarossa Coconut Rum

Barbarossa Mango Rum

Barbarossa Pineapple Coconut Rum

Barbarossa Spiced Rum

Baroca Dark Rum

Baroca Gold Rum

Baroca Silver Rum

Baroca Spiced Rum

Blu Fusion

Cabana Bay Coconut Rum

Cabana Bay Kiwi Strawberry Rum

Cabana Bay Mojito Rum

Cabana Bay Pineapple Coconut Rum

Cabana Bay Raspberry Rum

Cabana Bay Vanilla Spice Rum

Cabana Bay Wild Cherry Rum

Calico Jack Silver Rum

Calico Jack Spiced Rum

California Brand

Canadian Regal

Canadian Reserve

Chateau Monet Black Raspberry Liqueur

Chateau Pomari Pomegranate Liqueur

Chila Coffee Liqueur

Chymes Canadian Whisky

De Corso

Destinee

Destinee Ruby

Dimitri Gin

Dimitri Rum

Dimitri Vodka

E'Dolce Amaretto

El Chico Tequila

Fire Water Cinnamon Schnapps

Francesca Hazelnut Liqueur

Galens Vodka

Gold Crown Coffee Brandy

Gold Crown Rum

Gold Crown Vodka

Gold Crown Whisky

Gold Rush Cinnamon Schnapps

White Rock Distilleries

Grand Macnish Blended Scotch Whisky

Grand Suzette

Granny's Sour Apple Schnapps

Graves Vodka

Hannah & Hogg Gin

Hannah & Hogg Rum

Hannah & Hogg Vodka

Jenkins Gin

Jenkins Rum

Jenkins Vodka

Jolly Apple Schapps

Jolly Butterscotch Schnapps

Jolly Grape Schnapps

Jolly Peach Schnapps

Jolly Pom Schnapps

Banana Jack Rum

Cherry Jack Rum

Coconut Jack Rum

Mango Jack Rum

Pineapple Coconut Jack Rum

Kolomyka Vodka

Lawerence Whiskey

Lawerence Vodka

Luxov Vodka

McClelland's Single Malt Highland

McClelland's Single Malt Islay

McClelland's Single Malt Lowland

McClelland's Single Malt speyside

Mexican Silver Tequila

Mount Royal Lite

Nuyens Vodka

Orloff Vodka

Orloff Citrus Vodka

Orloff Green Apple Vodka

Orloff Raspberry Vodka

Pinnacle Gin

Pinnacle Vodka

Pinnacle Apple Vodka

Pinnacle Banana Vodka

Pinnacle Berry Vodka

Pinnacle Blueberry Vodka

Pinnacle Cherry Vodka

Pinnacle Chocolate Vodka

Pinnacle Citrus Vodka

Pinnacle Espresso Vodka

Pinnacle Grape Vodka

Pinnacle Kiwi-Strawberry Vodka

Pinnacle Melon Vodka

Pinnacle Mango Vodka

Pinnacle Orange Vodka

Pinnacle Pomegranate Vodka

Pinnacle Raspberry Vodka

Pinnacle Vodka Vanilla

Poland Spring Vodka

Proska Vodka

White Rock Distilleries

Q Gin

Ron Virgin Dark

Ron Virgin Silver

Ryan's Irish Cream

Ryan's Cappuccino Cream

Screech Rum

Superia Vodka

Sutton Club Gin

Sutton Club Rum

Sutton Club Vodka

Sutton Club Whiskey

Sweet Carolina Sweet Tea Vodka

Tenure Vodka

Tenure Blueberry Vodka

Tenure Berry Vodka

Tenure Cherry Vodka

Tenure Grape Vodka

Tenure Raspberry Vodka

Tenure Butterscotch Vodka

Tenure Rootbeer Vodka

Tortilla Tequila Gold

Tortilla Tequila Silver

Tortilla Tequila Liqueur

Tropic Bay Rum

Vera Cruz Tequila

Volta Vodka

V. Vodka

V. Le Double Espresso Vodka

Zhenka Vodka

William Grant and Sons

Clan MacGregor

Glenfiddich Special Reserve 12 Year Old

Glenfiddich Solera Reserve 15 Year Old

Glenfiddich Ancient Reserve 18 Year Old

Glenfiddich Gran Reserva 21 Year Old

Glenfiddich 30 Year Old

Glenfiddich Vintage Reserve

Glenfiddich 40 Year Old

Glenfiddich 50 Year Old

Glenfiddich Rare Collection 1937

Grant's Scotch Whisky

Grant's Family Reserve

Grant's Sherry Cask Reserve

Hendrick's Gin

Lillet

Milagro Limon Tequila

Milagro Mandarina Tequila

Milagro Silver

Milagro Reposado

Milagro Select Barrel Reserve Silver

Milagro Anejo

Milagro Select Barrel Reserve Reposado

Milagro Select Barrel Reserve Anejo

Reyka Vodka

Raynal

William Grant and Sons

Raynal VSOP

Raynal XO

Raynal Cranberry

Raynal VSOP

Raynal XO

Raynal Cranberry

Sailor Jerry Spiced Rum

The Balvenie DoubleWood 12 Year Old®

The Balvenie PortWood 1991®

The Balvenie Single Barrel 15 Year Old®

The Balvenie PortWood 21 Year Old®

The Balvenie® Thirty

The Balvenie Vintage Cask

More than a few people made this book possible but here's a short list of people that were vital to its creation:

Siska McClure
Alanna McClure
Nick McClure
Sam Howard
Michael Lane
Dariel
Stephanie Huang/Doll
Darby C. Doll
Paul Bisson
Liv Lo
Eric Williams
Matt Flint
Shadow Armstrong

CHEERS!

May we never want for a friend, or a bottle to give him.

- Charles Dickens, 19th Century English Writer

MY RECIPES

May our friendship, like wine, improve with time

Away with farewells,
Let welcomes always be!
And may we always share wells
Of friendship deep as sea!

Come, fill to joyous years,
This crystal clear and fine-
The morn may fill with tears,
What now we fill with wine!

- Herman Sheffauer, Early 20th Century American Poet